THE QUINTESSENCE OF THE ANIMATE AND INANIMATE

Frank Elliot (Karma Sangye Chupal)

H. H. Karmapa

This book is dedicated to His Holiness the Sixteenth Gyalwa Karmapa, Rangjung Rikpe Dorje, Head of the Kagyu Lineage, who is considered comparable only to the Buddha Shakyamuni in his understanding of the Three Times. To our great sorrow, this profound and compassionate teacher left this life several years ago and is sorely missed. His disciples wish for the rapid return of his Dharmakaya to human form.

THE QUINTESSENCE OF THE ANIMATE AND INANIMATE

A Discourse on the Holy Dharma

by
Venerable Lama Lodö

Foreword by
The Very Venerable Kalu Rinpoche

KDK PUBLICATIONS
San Francisco
1985

Published by KDK Publications
San Francisco, California
Printed in the United States of America

Library of Congress Cataloging in Publication Data

Lodru, Lama.
   The quintessence of the animate and inanimate.

   Bibliography: p.
   Includes index.
   1. Spiritual life (Buddhism)   2. Buddhism—China—Tibet—
Doctrines.   I. Title.
BQ5660.L63   1985   294.3'42   85-2290
ISBN 0-910165-01-7

Cover Drawing: Kyung-po Naljor, a Tibetan contemporary of
Gampopa and founder of the Shangpa Kagyu lineage, studied
under 150 Indian gurus. From his four main gurus, Niguma,
Rahula, Bebe Naljor, and Sukhasiddhi, he received many profound dharma teachings which he brought back to Tibet. He
established a monastery in Shang where he transmitted these
teachings, laying the groundwork for a lineage which has produced many great yogis and practitioners of the Dharma.

ISBN 0-910165-01-7

To order copies of this book, contact:
KDK PUBLICATIONS
1892 Fell Street
San Francisco, CA 94117

Contents

The Very Venerable Kalu Rinpoche
wearing the ceremonial Gampopa Hat.
Photograph taken at Kagyu Ling Retreat Center, Plaige, France.

Foreward

I would like to acquaint all those people whose support for the Buddhadharma derives from noble aspirations and positive karmic connections, with this work written by my disciple Lama Lodö. In writing *The Quintessence of the Animate and Inanimate,* he has wished to benefit others, and these words of Lama Lodö can be considered authentic and in accordance with the Dharma as taught by the Buddha; some teachings are presented from each of the three yanas. In the hope that everyone will benefit greatly from this work, I ask all concerned to approach it with this in mind. I speak as one who regards all traditions of the Buddha's teachings with the utmost respect.

Samdrub Thargay Ling Monastery
P.O. Sonada 734219
Darjeeling, W. Bengal
India

Preface

It was in the fall of 1974 after a public meditation that I first met the Venerable Kalu Rinpoche in California. Rinpoche mentioned to me that he intended to start a dharma center in the San Francisco area. "It would be beneficial if you could help my students in starting that center, and perhaps even live in it," he said. Two months later Rinpoche returned to San Francisco and a new dharma center, Kagyu Droden Kunchab, was born. He promised to send us a qualified lama to provide teachings and spiritual guidance.

Exactly two years later, in 1976, his representative Lama Lodö arrived at K.D.K. Since that time, Lama Lodö has provided extensive teachings in Buddhist practices and philosophy, with special emphasis on the Vajrayana traditions of Tibet. 6 A.M. and 8 P.M. meditations are performed daily, seven days a week, every day of the year. On weekends, there are two extra sessions at 10 A.M. On Saturday evenings, unless he is out of town, Lama Lodö conducts a question and answer session with those who have attended the 8 P.M. Chenrezig Puja. Every month during the full moon period, he conducts the two-day Nyung Nes retreat. Once each year he has led participants on the Eight Nyung Nes retreat (sixteen days) and given the Amitabha Powa instructions on the concluding two days. For the last two years during the summer months, he has given a three-week retreat on Chöd and Mahakala practices. And, all during these years, Lama Lodö would give periodic lecture series on various dharma topics requested by interested students. (The recordings of some of those teachings, which were accumulated over a number of years, are the basis of this book.) All these activities are in addition to the personal instructions given to his students on a daily basis. Under his guidance, the center has undergone a remarkable increase in active membership and satellite centers have been opened in communities surrounding San Francisco as well as in Eugene, Oregon.

When he arrived in San Francisco, the center's premises were being rented. Through his inspiration and careful management of resources, K.D.K.'s home is now being purchased. Also, in Oregon, a Three Year Retreat facility is being constructed and it is expected that between fifteen and twenty people will begin the traditional Three Year-Three Month Retreat this year. Lama Tsewang Tsering, a qualified retreat leader appointed by Kalu Rinpoche himself, will conduct the retreat.

Since 1978, I have worked closely with Lama Lodö as his president of K.D.K. The object lessons learned in this position have at times been as difficult to swallow as cod-liver oil. The value of strong medicine is usually difficult to apprehend without the benefit of hindsight. Now, looking back, it is more clear to me how Lama Lodö's vision and use of skillful means carried Rinpoche's center from where it was in 1976 to where it is in 1985. The Venerable Kalu Rinpoche has often said that the most supreme way to repay the kindness of your teachers is through dedicated practice of the Buddha Dharma. For me, their kindness seems impossible to repay. However, as I too prepare to enter the Three Year Retreat, I pray that through the blessings of the lineage and my kind root Lama, the result of my meager practice will be the benefit of all sentient beings in whatever realm, in whatever time.

Michael Conklin (Karma Sönam Rinchen)
President, Kagyu Droden Kunchab
San Francisco
February, 1985

Publisher's Note

One doesn't always walk into the Dharma. Some of us stumble rather clumsily into it, poking our heads in ever so slightly with curiosity and both a willingness and an unwillingness to take the teachings as true.

I fell, literally, into the Dharma on a dusty road in Norway in 1976, having just met Lama Lodö for the first time.

Three years later, in San Francisco, he handed me a shoebox which contained KDK Publications. He told me it was my responsibility and to take care of it. Lama Lodö was patient and strict and the interesting part of his teachings was to experience them directly in daily life.

KDK Publications grew to closet size and I had more responsibilities in the world with a full-time job and a husband. I often had questions arise in my practice, but Lama Lodö's answer to my questions was usually the same: "Meditate more." And so I did.

Nine years since that hot, dusty day in Norway, I am waiting for Three Year Retreat to begin. KDK Publications is bursting out of its closet with English translations of Tibetan texts, puja texts galore in both English transliteration and Tibetan, and Lama Lodö's continuing publications: *Attaining Enlightenment, Bardo Teachings,* and now *Quintessence of the Animate and Inanimate: A Discourse on the Holy Dharma.*

I dedicate whatever merit there has been to the benefit of

all sentient beings. As yet I cannot find how deep Lama Lodö is, because the deeper I go in my practice, the more depth there is in him that I cannot yet reach, and so I practice more. I am touched beyond words by how much he has cared and helped to guide me along this path.

May you, the reader, benefit from these teachings. I hope they bring you joy, peace, and understanding in your life, and open new doors of experience.

In the Dharma,
Kira Henriksen
KDK Publications Coordinator
San Francisco
February, 1985

Editor's Preface

The Kagyu lineage is firmly grounded in a tradition of oral transmission from teacher to student. It therefore seems particularly fitting that this book is based upon public talks given by Lama Lodö to his students over a period of several years. Anyone attending these teachings would have been deeply affected by Lama Lodö's vigorous and clear expression of the Dharma; his ability to transmit the meaning of this inexhaustible subject seems unlimited.

Each of these teachings was recorded and then transscribed at a later time. Our efforts as editors have been directed toward the "translation" from oral to written, and we hope that Lama Lodö's lively and skillful style have been accurately retained. Our colleague in this endeavor was Bill Voigt, who worked closely with Lama Lodö to faithfully maintain the precision of the teaching as it progressed from tape to printed page. His strength in the Tibetan language and his grasp of the concepts presented in this book were an invaluable resources for us throughout the project. We particularly appreciate his hard work on the rewriting of the "Methods of Meditation and Visualization" and "Viewing Emptiness" chapters.

In our early discussions with Lama Lodö about the format of *The Quintessence of the Animate and Inanimate,* he expressed his intention to create a book which would be a reference work. We feel that it is a strength of this book that anyone, from curious beginner to Buddhist scholar, can benefit from his knowledgeable and graduated presentation.

We want to thank Lama Lodö for the many hours he spent answering our questions and discussing the book with us. He is an insightful and generous teacher and we feel fortunate to be able to work with him.

We dedicate all merit resulting from our efforts to the enlightenment of all sentient beings.

Nancy Clark (Karma Pema Zangmo)
Caroline Parke (Karma Yeshe Chödron)
Kagyu Suka Chöling
Eugene, Oregon
February, 1985

Acknowledgements

Creating this book was the result of the efforts of many people. Transcribing of the original lecture tapes was done by Elizabeth Johnson (Karma Sönam Chödzom), Ruthanne Harris (Karma Tabka Pema), Karen Nelson (Karma Chökyi Drönma), Robyn Partridge (Karma Metok Lhamo), Catherine Travis (Karma Dawa Lhamo), Emmy Fox (Karma Sönam Lhatso), and Allen Carosio (Karma Chöying Gyatso).

The manuscript was typed by Martina Rosa, Ruthanne Harris, Karen Nelson, and Elizabeth Johnson. Ruthanne Harris also arranged much of the book production and Kira Henriksen provided financial coordination and support at KDK Publications.

Lama Lodö's manuscript review was aided by Bill Voigt (Karma Jinpa Tarchin), Bill Velton (Karma Tashi Nyima), and Michael Conklin (Karma Sönam Rinchen). The glossary was done by Bill Voigt and Michael Conklin.

Nancy Clark (Karma Pema Zangmo) and Caroline Parke (Karma Yeshe Chödron) were the editors for this book. As primary liaison with the editors, Bill Voigt worked on many of the details concerning book content with Lama Lodö.

Eloise Van Tassel (Karma Tenzin Zangmo) created the Kyung-po Naljor drawing. Tara Sullivan (Karma Drolma Chutso) drew the symbols which represent and introduce each of the Six Paramitas and Cari Cagle (Karma Drolkar Trinley) did the layout for the cover.

I wish to thank everyone for their many hours of hard work.

Introduction

When I was sixteen, I embarked upon a solitary retreat in a cave. Of course, I had a great spiritual teacher who guided me day by day and who provided me with understanding of the great Vajrayana Path; truly all that I understand is through his kindness. I also learned a lot at that time just through observing how the external world exists and how my own mind maintains itself from moment to moment.

When my mind is peaceful and gentle, I see all the inanimate world as the completely blissful realm. When my mind is emotionally upset, it leads me to the hell realms right there. So, back then, sitting in my cave for a long time, I came to know that all is produced from one's own mind.

Now I am writing ths book called *The Quintessence of the Animate and Inanimate*, because I realize through my experience that the animate and inanimate can produce both positive and negative. All mind and substance, by which I mean all living beings and the environment that supports them—the beings and the field of their actions—are, in conjunction, the essential factors determining our happiness and our suffering. So this discourse on the Holy Dharma is really the quintessence of the animate and inanimate and I hope that all my readers may benefit in increasing knowledge, merit, and happiness.

Lama Lodö
Kagyu Droden Kunchab
San Francisco
February, 1985

Section I:
Foundations

Chapter One
Four Foundations

The Four Foundations are sometimes called "the four thoughts which turn the mind" because contemplation of them will turn us away from worldly interests and toward the road to enlightenment. They are the base upon which the Dharma is built.

Dharma is a Sanskrit word meaning "truth." In general it refers to all phenomena, both samsara and nirvana. Samsaric dharma is that which leads to involvement in all the worldly activities, and these in turn lead one to sink further into samsara. The Holy Dharma leads one out of and away from samsara.

There are two categories of the Holy Dharma, the Dharma of Precept and the Dharma of Realization. The Dharma of Precept is that which was presented by Buddha Shakyamuni as the 84,000 dharma teachings. These are the antidotes to the 84,000 conflicting emotions. When we follow these precepts, learn, meditate on them, achieve understanding of them, and then come to some experience of their truth through our practice, this is called the Dharma of Realization.

The Buddha Shakyamuni was the great being in our Age who elucidated these truths, the nature of pure mind, and the method through which we might attain it. He lived in

3

India in the fifth century B.C. and achieved the state of complete enlightenment before reaching middle age. In his remaining years, he taught others what was required to escape from the cycle of samsara and to achieve a state of complete enlightenment exactly as he had done.

The necessity for each human being to follow the path to enlightenment is contained in the teachings on the Four Foundations. These are the simple principles which make meaningful every moment of our lives and they are always presented first to remind us of the vital importance of our journey. The chapters which follow lay down some of the steps we can take on that path.

Precious Human Existence

All sentient beings, that is, those beings who have sense perceptions, have Buddha nature, and this is the seed of enlightenment. We see this Buddha nature in the smallest insects and organisms, which react to life as we do, by running from pain and running toward pleasure. It is difficult to imagine any being that would not want to better itself by decreasing pain and increasing pleasure, but very few beings have the power to do so. The human being is particularly fortunate, then, to have not only Buddha nature but also the potential to make life better. In fact, it is only the human being who can attain the ultimate reformation, enlightenment. Only the human being has access to the favorable circumstances that are necessary for this arduous journey.

Buddha nature may be compared to a rice seed. If it is planted in poor soil and not given enough water and sunlight, it cannot reach healthy maturity. If, however, it is planted in good soil and is given enough water and sunlight to nurture it, it will grow to a mature plant whose fruits will feed many.

Buddha nature needs many favorable conditions to grow to this same kind of maturity. These conditions are called the Eight Freedoms and the Ten Endowments; it is these eighteen qualities that make human existence "precious."

The first of the Eight Freedoms is to be free from life in the hell realms where physical and mental suffering is so excruciating and constant that beings have no chance to think of dharma or virtue or getting enlightened. In this realm, every being is in agony every minute. The second freedom is not living in the hungry ghost realms where constant hunger and thirst overpower any thought of spiritual practice. Third is the freedom from the animal realms where stupidity and ignorance block the understanding of virtue and where evil habits prevail.

It is very rare for humans to see the hell or hungry ghost realms, but we are all familiar with the animal realm. We can see that there is no understanding of the difference between harmful and beneficial deeds nor any disciplined effort to achieve distant goals.

Fourth, the precious human is free of life in the god realms where temporary blissful pleasures encourage laziness and eradicate the desire to practice virtue. Living in the god realms would be much like earning $10,000 and then quitting work. You would live an existence of luxury and ease, with no thought for tomorrow, until the money was gone and then suddenly you would come down to reality with a crash. Living in the god realms is the result of good karma in past lives, but this state of pleasurable reward always comes to a sudden end. Since the gods do not use their lives for virtue, their laziness will produce suffering and future rebirth in the lower realms.

Compared to the suffering of beings in these four realms, the suffering of the human realm can be valuable. Humans can be motivated by their own misery to improve their lives. Humans can also feel compassion for the pain of others and can act to lessen that suffering. Finally, human beings can feel loving kindness toward others and can act to benefit them. Without suffering, human beings would exist in a kind of god realm, living only for the pleasures of today and having no thought for the future or for anyone else's wellbeing.

The remaining freedoms concern the human realm. The fifth freedom is to be free from life in a "barbaric" country. This describes a life without high moral principles, where humans live by killing and stealing. Humans in a barbaric country lack teachers and practitioners of good habits and therefore have no hope of enlightenment.

The sixth freedom is to be free from "wrong views." Human beings who have access to teachers and practitioners and who refuse to believe in suffering, cause and effect, and enlightenment, are those who cling to wrong views. They throw away their opportunity for enlightenment by refusing to believe in its necessity and reality.

The seventh freedom is to be exempt from life in a dark time when no enlightened beings appear. Naturally, if there is no one to show the path, humans become unknowing, just like animals.

The eighth freedom is to be free from obstacles to the communication and understanding of the spiritual path. These obstacles include being blind, deaf, dumb, and having mental deficiency or illness.

If you are reading this book and able to understand it, you are fortunate enough to be blessed with the Eight Freedoms. You possess the leisure and opportunity to walk the path to enlightenment since your life has these favorable circumstances.

The second set of conditions governing precious human existence is called the Ten Endowments. The first five are gifts we provide for ourselves; the remaining five are gifts which come from others. First, we have been born human beings by virtue of our own actions in previous lives. Second, we have been born in a country where the dharma is flourishing and this is due to a habitual tendency to pursue the dharma in previous lives. Third, our senses, organs, and mind are perfect as a result of avoiding destructive actions and performing virtuous actions in earlier lives.

Fourth, we hold right views and this is due to our earlier habits of being devoted to the enlightened ones, feeling compassion for the sufferings of sentient beings, and avoiding harmful deeds. Fifth, we have the habit of faith and confidence in enlightened beings. We know them, from the habit of many lifetimes, to be completely pure and full of great wisdom, infinite compassion, and flawless loving kindness. Based on these habits, we respect the Buddha Shakyamuni, who is the enlightened being of this age; we respect his teachings, the Dharma, which are the path to enlightenment; and we respect the Sangha, the practitioners who guide us on this path.

Our bodies have died many times in many realms, but our minds have never died. The memory and results of our previous virtuous actions are seen in these first five endowments.

The remaining endowments are those which are gifts from others. The first is the appearance of the Buddha and other enlightened beings in this world. It is their compassion for sentient beings which brings them here. Second, the Buddha gave teachings which elucidate the path to enlightenment. He attained that state of complete awakening, and through his compassion, he realized that all beings should be able to have that kind of liberation. Third, the teachings remain in the world. They are accurate and available for our use.

Fourth, there are many people following the path to enlightenment. We are fortunate to have companions and teachers to guide us. Fifth and last, there are generous donors who support the practitioners through gifts of money and materials. As with each of these last five endowments, the gifts of donors do not come to any human being through their own efforts or desires, but through the compassion and loving kindness of others.

Those who enjoy the Eight Freedoms and Ten Endowments have a precious human existence. It is said to be "difficult to obtain and easily lost." How difficult it is to obtain this precious human existence may be understood by the use of a comparison. Imagine that our world is composed entirely of water and a wooden yoke is floating aimlessly upon its surface. A blind turtle, rising to some random point on that surface just once every hundred years, would have a greater chance of placing its head in that yoke that any being has of obtaining a precious human existence! In this analogy, the ocean represents our samsaric world of suffering, the turtle stands for all sentient beings, and its blindness represents beings' ignorance of the causes of happiness and suffering. The yoke is a symbol of Dharma teachings.

Our human existence is also more valuable than the proverbial wish-fulfilling gem. This jewel, which can satisfy every worldly request we might make of it, still cannot give us the permanent happiness of enlightenment toward which a precious human existence alone can lead.

It is natural for sentient beings to act harmfully rather than beneficially, and it is exceedingly difficult to act sufficiently virtuously over the many lifetimes required to cause the result of human rebirth. If a human also is blessed with the great opportunities inherent in being near the Dharma, then no moment of that precious human existence should be wasted.

In addition to being difficult to obtain, the precious human existence is easy to lose. Even the most well-endowed life is precarious. We never know when our bodies will fade or when accidents may occur. This looming awareness of death is yet another motivation for dedicating ourselves to the path of enlightenment.

When we dedicate ourselves to this quest for enlightenment, there are three attributes which, when added to the Eight Freedoms and the Ten Endowments, form the perfect vessel for enlightenment. These attributes are forms of devotion. It says in the sutras that "without devotion, wholesome human deeds are impossible." The mind which lacks devotion is likened to a seed that is rotten at the core. Even if it is planted, it cannot sprout or grow a healthy plant.

Buddha advised his disciple Ananda to apply devotion in order to release suffering. When Ananda asked for more detail, Buddha described three kinds of devotion: belief, longing, and uncontrived devotion. All three are important elements on the spiritual path.

The devotion that springs from belief is that which trusts the relationship between actions and their results. This is the principle which states that our present lives are the result of past actions and our future lives will be the result of present actions. We are motivated to do virtuous actions, knowing that they lead to rebirth as a human or god, and to avoid nonvirtuous actions, knowing that they lead to rebirth in the lower realms.

The devotion that springs from longing is that which views the Buddha and other enlightened beings as having achieved a level of bliss, independence, compassion, and wisdom that we also would like to achieve. We become devoted to the path in order to achieve this goal.

Uncontrived devotion is inspired by the Three Jewels. We see the awakened state of the Buddha, we hear his words about the path to enlightenment in the Dharma, and we see that message as it is lived by the Sangha. All of these inspire us to seek the state of clear mind.

If we feel these three forms of devotion, we must take

care not to be distracted by the four obstacles of desire, anger, fear, and ignorance. Desire for possessions or temporary happiness, anger at sentient beings, fear of the consequences of our actions, or ignoring the laws of action and result, can be serious distractions from the path to enlightenment, especially after we have begun our journey. We must endeavor to remain devoted to the path.

The full combination of Eight Freedoms, Ten Endowments, and three forms of devotion constitutes the perfect vessel for enlightenment. Some of the benefits of a lifetime as this perfect vessel are that it is easy to do beneficial deeds, the incidence of conflicting emotions decreases, and the enlightened beings will influence you. These beings are attracted to the rare event of a perfect vessel and they will affect your teachings or actually appear to teach you.

For the seed of Buddhahood to grow to maturity requires the precious human existence filled with Eight Freedoms, Ten Endowments, and three kinds of devotion. This combination constitutes the perfect vessel for enlightenment which is an opportunity that is infinitely rare and should not be wasted.

Impermanence

The Buddha said that all composite phenomena are impermanent. He described this truth in four ways: all things that are gathered, such as wealth and possessions, will be exhausted; all things that stand, such as trees and houses, will fall; all meetings will end in separation; and all things that are born will die.

There are three elements in this discussion of impermanence: categories, methods, and benefit. The categories are impermanence in the external world and impermanence in the internal world. The internal world is defined as all sentient beings; the external world is defined as what is all around those beings.

The external world is viewed in two ways, a general explanation and a detailed one. The general explanation given here is the traditional Buddhist view of the world. There is a wind mandala which supports this world and the four levels of samadhi gods above it. This world and the first three levels of samadhi gods will someday be destroyed. The cause of this destruction will be the element of fire which will consume this world and the first level of gods as completely as butter is consumed in a hot pan. Then the wind mandala will fill the empty space and the world will be re-formed. It will next be destroyed by the element water up to the second level of samadhi gods as completely as salt dissolves in water. The wind mandala will fill empty space again and the world will re-form. This time it will be destroyed by the element wind, including the third level of gods, as completely as sand is dispersed by wind.

The fourth level of samadhi gods is exempt from this process. The world and god levels below this highest one are formed by collective karma and suffer collective results. At the fourth level, each god is living its individual karma with individual phenomena. When a god dies, all its phenomena or worldly appearances die with it. The conclusion of this general explanation is that the world at every level, whether collective or individual, is constantly dying.

The detailed explanation of external world impermanence concerns the world around us. Nature, which may appear to be static, is in fact governed by the changing seasons. Many living things will sprout or be born in the spring, grow in the summer, drop seeds in the autumn, and die in the winter. Even those beings which live longer than a year are strongly affected by the seasons' change. For many in the animal realm, spring is the time of birth and winter the time of hibernation, and even human beings' moods and endeavors are affected by the seasons.

We may view the predictability of the cycle and conclude that each year is changeless, the same as the last. However, the reminder of impermanence is in the evidence of aging which we see in ourselves and every living being as each year passes.

The fluctuation of day and night also reflects the constancy of change. If the phenomenal world were changeless, we would live in endless daylight or endless darkness. The passing of day and night remind us of the passing of time.

Finally we see impermanence in each moment of the present which was once a moment of the future and soon will be part of the past. Each moment is quickly exhausted and can never exist again.

Normally, moments of time are passing by so continuously that their very passing may appear to be constant. To correct that perception, we can look at a waterfall. It appears to be a steady stream of water but actually it is millions of tiny individual droplets, each one falling. Time may appear to be a steady stream also, but actually it is millions of tiny individual events, each one happening and ending. Each event, each moment, is a life and death, and will never stay or return.

We also have evidence of impermanence from our internal world. As sentient beings, we were born and will die. We have the deaths of the beings who preceeded us to show us this, and we know that beings around us continue to die every day. We know of no being who has defeated death, no matter how brave or smart or determined they may have been.

The Buddha said that all beings are like clouds on a windy autumn day. One moment we are here, then we are blown away, and then we return. So we are born, we die, and we are reborn. We cannot stop or alter this process, nor can we control how our deaths will happen.

When we look at impermanence and death, we can become motivated to take advantage of the rare event of our precious human existence. Our impending deaths can encourage us to alter our habits of clinging to temporary worldly habits and can engender new habits of seeking permanent happiness in full enlightenment.

The category of the internal world is viewed in two ways: We look at ourselves and apply what we learn to others and we look at others and apply it to ourselves. We begin by seriously acknowledging the inevitable result of living which is our own deaths. Second, we contemplate the characteristics of our own deaths. We will feel tremendous terror at the exhaustion of our life force and the loss of our breathing. We will become corpses, abhorrent objects to those around us, and our bodies will be removed to "places of rest" under the ground. Simultaneously, our consciousnesses are separated from our bodies and we wander fearful and alone in that terrifying state between life and death. Once we have reached the time of our deaths, it is far too late for regret or improvement of our actions.

Next we contemplate the continual exhausting of life. Each moment that passes is a moment less in the length of our lives; the amount of life left to us today will be lessened by twenty-four hours tomorrow. Our lives decrease every second and can only end in death.

Finally, we contemplate the separations brought about by death. All our accumulated possessions and wealth, our parents, spouses, and children will be left behind. When death comes, we have no choice but to separate. We go alone and naked into a future we cannot predict.

It is at this point in the discussion of the internal world that the category of method is addressed. This is a method for meditating on our own impermanence and its basis is three statements: "I am certainly dying;" "I am unsure when my death will happen;" and, "When my death comes, nothing can stop it, just as nothing can stop the sun from sinking in the west." Each of these statements has three companion thoughts which form a total of nine parts of the meditation.

The first contemplation when we consider the certainty of our own deaths is that all beings who have ever lived have died. Even the highest beings—Mahasiddhas and teachers who could perform great miracles such as flying and appearing in many places at once—have all left their bodies at death. If these great ones die, how much more likely it is that we will die?

The second contemplation concerning our own certain deaths is the recognition that our bodies are formed by the skandhas. It is therefore impossible that we should live permanently because the nature of the skandhas is destructibility.

The final meditation on our own predictable deaths is the fact that life is exhausted each second. We grow older every year and years are composed of seconds. An analogy is drawn between our lives and an arrow loosed from a bow. Once released, the arrow can do nothing but fall; once we are born, we can do nothing but die. Another analogy is made to people being led to execution. Each step brings them closer to their appointment with death, and our lives are much the same. We have all been sentenced to die.

When we consider the statement, "I am unsure when my death will occur," the first contemplation is that death can happen at any age. Some beings die in the womb and some in extreme old age; some die of illness and some from sudden accident. We cannot depend on living a long life.

The second meditation on the uncertain time of death is that our bodies cannot avoid death due to their composition. We have no physical protections against death. Every element of our bodies is failing from the moment we are born and any single component can cause us to die in an instant.

The final contemplation of the unpredictible time of our deaths is that we cannot know or control the cause of our deaths. The sage Nagarjuna said that our lives were like candles burning in the wind or like water bubbles. To inhale after we exhale, to awaken after we sleep, are wonderful opportunities which we can lose at any moment.

The third statement, "When the time of my death comes, nothing can save me," leads us to contemplate wealth and possessions. The things we accumulate in this life are no barrier to death. In fact, clinging to them can add to our desperate wish not to die and can be the source of avoiding the pursuit of spiritual matters. Seeking wealth and possessions fosters the conflicting emotions of greed, desire, jealousy, pride, anger, and ignorance. It is a source, at best, of temporary happiness and, at worst, of rebirth in the lower realms.

The second meditation on our lack of protection from death concerns relatives and friends. These people, over whom we agonize during our whole lives, are the source of only temporary happiness and still cannot stand between us and death. They are a cause of the conflicting emotions in us and therefore, our interactions can lead to a lower rebirth.

The last contemplation on our vulnerability to death is that our own bodies cannot save us at the moment of death. Our body qualities of strength and quickness cannot stay death and our body's essence will confuse and hamper us at that time. We spend our lives caring for our bodies and suddenly, at death, we are separated from them. Our attachment to the body makes death seem worse and can be a source of lower rebirth.

When we use this method of meditation or when we view ourselves as part of the internal world, it is important to apply these thoughts and conclusions to others. This can be a source of compassion and also a motivation to share our concerns about utilizing this life to the fullest spiritual potential.

We return to the discussion the internal world by focusing our attention on others and applying what we learn to ourselves. The first step is to see that others die. Most of us have known someone who seemed favored by life. They might have been beautiful or wise or full of youth and good spirits. Suddenly they caught some disease or had an accident and they changed dramatically. Their beauty or wisdom or youth rapidly faded; their body and personality changed into something uncomfortable and unhappy. When we see these events, we must remember that this will happen to us.

Second, when we hear of someone's death we must think more than, "Oh, I'm sorry that person is gone." We can apply their death more personally and add, "That person is my teacher. Someday someone will say that I have died. Before that happens, I should do beneficial deeds and prepare for my death." The teacher Shantideva once said, "The next moment or the next life? We don't know which will come first." We should prepare now for the next life instead of putting it off until tomorrow, for we may not have a tomorrow.

Our last view of others' deaths is always to remember that people have died. The deaths of all the friends and relatives we've known and all the famous people we've heard about can be a continuous reminder and motivation for us to practice.

The final category, benefits, addresses what effects the doctrine of impermanence can have on us if we understand it. Acknowledging the impermanence of life can reduce our attachment to the world and make us more devoted to the enlightened ones. We also become more diligent in our practice and achieve some separation from the conflicting emotions. Without an understanding of the doctrine of impermanence, no other teachings will be helpful to us.

As sentient beings, we contain the seed of Buddhahood and the seed of death. Acknowledging the seed of death turns us toward the seed of Buddhahood; understanding impermanence leads us to utilize our precious human existence. The yogi Milarepa said, "I was afraid of death so I escaped to the mountain. Now I am no longer afraid. I welcome death." Fear of his own death led him to diligent mountain retreat. He was an ordinary being who achieved Buddhahood, the state beyond death.

Faults of Samsara

There may be times when we think that this human existence is just fine, and we assume that we will come back in future lives and continue to improve ourselves. At other times this life may seem so terrible that we think of ending it, and we assume that the next one will have to be better. The assumptions that we will continue being reborn as humans and that future lives will be better ones are erroneous and this must obviously alter our plans for the life we now are leading.

Attaining a human existence is a tremendously rare event. The number of denizens in the five other realms is variously described as being like atoms on earth or grains of sand or snowflakes in the sky. The precious human existence is described as being "rare as daytime stars."

Clinging to the assumption of continued human rebirth is an obstacle of confidence. We look upon birth in the human or god realms as something automatically attractive, much as children may be attracted to a fire. However, life in the higher realms may be every bit as painful as jumping into a fire. We know this to be true if we think about the sorrows of this world, and we will be even more motivated to pursue enlightenment if we understand the sorrows of all the other realms.

The reality of our situation is that it has taken much hard work to attain this life. Even if we have our health and mental faculties and are free from want, this life contains many miseries which we cannot escape. Investigating and accepting this reality can awaken us to the necessity to do something about it.

All six realms have three kinds of suffering. The first is "the suffering of composition" and this is the source of all suffering. It is the potential for all misery and may be compared to fruit which is not yet ripe enough to be eaten, yet holds within it potential flavor, nourishment, and the seeds for future fruits.

The suffering of composition is the result of combining the five skandhas (form, feeling, perception, intention, consciousness) and the five elements (earth, air, fire, water, ether). This composition produces bodily reality and simultaneously produces the potential for suffering.

The suffering of composition causes only a neutral feeling in humans because we are not subtle enough to perceive it. The great teacher Gampopa said that we humans are like hands, enlightened beings are like eyes, and the suffering of composition is like dust. When dust settles on a hand, it is not even noticed; when it settles in an eye, it is impossible not to notice it. We cannot feel the subtle effects of the suffering of composition, which is like dust on a hand; the enlightened ones feel tremendous pain with the suffering of composition, which is like dust in an eye.

The second type of suffering is "the suffering of change" and it may be compared to exquisite fruit which contains poison. We are attracted to the fruit and have the rich experience of eating it, but this is followed by pain and possibly by death.

The suffering of change causes an initially blissful feeling, which is followed by pain or sorrow. An example of this experience is when we are attracted to someone and we go out on our first date. We have a wonderful time and are completely attached to them, thinking of them every moment. How crushed we are when we learn that they really don't care for us at all! The suffering of change is the prevalent form of suffering in the three higher realms of humans, jealous gods, and desire gods.

The third kind of suffering is "the suffering of suffering" and it is the easiest to see and understand. In our world, grinding poverty, famine, and starvation are all examples of the suffering of suffering. This type of suffering is particularly prevalent in the lower three realms of hell beings, hungry ghosts, and animals.

The suffering of suffering produces feelings of pain and sorrow. When we work to remove misery from our lives, we begin with the gross level, the suffering of suffering. When we have worked through that, we will be able to deeply feel the suffering of change. Only after we have cured this suffering of change will we be able to feel the suffering of composition.

Suffering is the major fault of samsara, the cycle of rebirth. We will look at each of the six realms to see the particular forms of suffering in each.

The hell realms consist of eight hot and eight cold hells and is the result of anger in former lives. Life is passed in interminable suffering of pains such as being killed many times each day, being born in fire, or being cooked on melting copper. Each lifetime is many times longer than our own. These sentient beings are obviously unable to think of anything beyond their own misery and are unable to devote any time to the Dharma. They remain in the hell realms until their karma is exhausted.

There has long been a philosophical discussion about the hell realms. Some scholars believe that it actually exists and some feel that it is an illusion produced by the human sinful mind. In either case, the experience of timeless agony without rescue is a powerful example of the suffering of suffering.

The hungry ghost realm is the result of greed and desire in former lives. These sentient beings suffer in one of three ways. Some want food and drink but never get any. All that they see turns into something inedible like blood. Others have huge stomachs, small necks, and mouths like the eye of a needle. They have difficulty getting to food and when they do, they can't swallow it. Still others can find and eat scraps of food but it turns into blazing fire in their mouths. They suffer with this pain until their karma is exhausted. All the miseries in these realms are less than those in the hell realms.

These beings live for five hundred years, and one month of human time is only one day in the hungry ghost realm. During all this time, misery totally preoccupies every being and there is no time for the Dharma.

The animal realms are the only other realms that most human beings can see. Birth in these realms is the result of ignorance in former lives. In many parts of our world, domesticated animals are treated terribly as beasts of burden or they are raised to be slaughtered. Some wild animals are hunted for their skin or flesh or horns and nearly all the animals and ocean creatures live in fear of being attacked and eaten by others. Many animals also suffer great pains when their bodies are the home for parasites.

Even the most fortunate domestic animal suffers from stupidity. Some animals lead lives many times longer than ours and some live incredibly short lives. In either case the difficulty of sustaining life and the necessity to constantly fight or kill to remain alive consumes each being's entire attention. In this realm, there is no knowledge of good or bad and therefore no chance for fortunate rebirth.

The human realm holds the sufferings of birth, old age, sickness, and death. Birth in this realm is the result of desire in other lives. The sufferings of birth actually begin with the sufferings of rebirth which precede the time in the womb. Our time in the bardo (intermediate states between one life and the next) is terrifying, and as we reach the end, our past actions will govern our rebirth. We have no "choice" at the time of conception but merely a series of cloudy perceptions.* One of these is attraction to our mothers and anger at our fathers if we will be born male. If we will be born female, we will feel attraction for our fathers and anger at our mothers.

We may think of birth as a joyous experience, but from the baby's perspective, the time in the womb and during birth is very painful and frightening. In the first week, the baby feels roasted on a copper pan and looks like watery yogurt. The second week, the baby has its four elements and looks like thick yogurt. In the third week, the baby feels its elemental energies awakening and it looks like an ant. For the next three weeks, it grows more awake and more sorrowful.

In the seventh week, the baby is forming arms and legs. This process feels as if a strong man were pulling them out of the baby's body. This continues for four weeks and includes the growth of feet and hands. In the eleventh week, the nine openings of the body are made, and from this time, the baby is very sensitive. It feels every change in the mother's environment. When the mother is cold, the baby is icy; when the mother overeats, the baby feels crushed;

---

*A complete explanation of the rebirth sequence appears in *Bardo Teachings, The Way of Death and Rebirth* by Venerable Lama Lodö. Revised Edition, KDK Publications, 1982.

when the mother walks fast, the baby feels like it is bouncing on rocks; when the mother is sad, the baby feels miserable.

By the thirty-seventh week, the womb feels dark and smelly and the baby wants to leave. The next week, the baby turns around and tries to get out. The mother's contractions cause the baby much pain, and if the baby survives the birth, the world is full of blinding light, freezing cold, and rough handling of its paper-thin skin. When we view birth from this perspective, we must ask ourselves, "Even if I could get back to this realm again, would I really want to go through that birth process?"

Most human lives include old age. At this time we become ugly and lose our strength, our memory, and our brightness. No one comes to visit us; we are lonely and sad. Remembering old age can motivate us to practice while we are young and have the physical and mental strength to learn discipline. Meditation will bring us peace in our old age.

When sickness strikes, we become "human hungry ghosts." We suffer seven ways: We have pain with our illness and pain from our treatment, we dislike our medicines, we are forbidden our favorite foods, we are dependent on our doctor, we worry that all our money will be spent on our illness, and we fear we will die from being sick.

Death is the unavoidable fact of life. It brings us pain, fear of the future, rupture from our past, and terrifying separation from our bodies.

In addition to these four major sufferings of human existence, we suffer in some other ways. We all have fears for our loved ones and we hate separations from them. We also fear and experience many calamities in this life. Finally, we seek to secure possessions all our lives and it is painful to fail or succeed at this, since we cannot hold on to anything forever.

Birth in the demi-god realm is the result of jealousy in former lives. It is full of sentient beings who enjoy great riches and pleasures. They are jealous of each other, however, and spend their entire existence fighting. This leaves no time for pursuing the path to enlightenment.

The desire god realm has riches without the drawback of constant fighting. Birth in this realm is the result of pride in former lives. However, after eons of heedless pleasure that seem to pass very quickly, they will suddenly awaken to the realization of death. The everlasting blossoms that ornament them fade and die and their bodies give off a sour smell. The other gods leave the dying one alone in the cemetery for the seven days preceeding death, which will seem longer to that god than the eons of pleasure which preceded it. These seven days will be the same as seven hundred human years.

During that long final week, the god experiences decay and realizes that all its good karma is exhausted so it will inevitably be reborn in a lower realm. It can see that future life and thus will suffer it in advance as it decays. The desire gods have had eons of leisure and well-being with which to consider virtue and enlightenment, but the seemingly endless pleasures erase motivation and necessity. The desire gods believed they had achieved the highest goal—until they felt death upon them.

We can see from this investigation that we must take advantage of this very lifetime. The human realm offers a unique opportunity: There is widespread suffering to motivate us to overcome samsara, but if we have attained a precious human existence, our own suffering is not so constant as to preclude the accomplishment of liberating actions. These include virtuous deeds, good bodily actions, meditation, mantras, visualizations, etc. The chief danger is that we will interpret our relative ease and relative lack of suffering as a kind of "human desire god realm" and blindly pursue our pleasures while ignoring our impending deaths. If we throw this opportunity away, how can we expect to return to so fortunate an existence? We must use the temporary pleasures as motivation to seek the permanent happiness of escaping samsara.

The Buddha and other enlightened beings are independent of samsara. They can choose to manifest in any realm to benefit beings. For us to truly benefit ourselves— and others—we too must become independent of samsara. Remembering the great sufferings of all the realms and dedicating our efforts to their needs will keep our practice in the proper perspective and protect us from obstacles.

Karma

The suffering in samsara is caused by the law of karma. This Sanskrit word means "action" and is more broadly translated as "cause and effect." If we know about the law of cause and effect, then we know we have a choice about the actions of our lives; if we do not know about the law, we will be affected by it out of ignorance.

Simply stated, the law of karma is that each virtuous act has virtuous results and each nonvirtuous act has nonvirtuous results. We reap the results of every action in this life or a future one. The Buddha stated that all external existence is the manifestation of karma and all sentient beings have individual levels of suffering brought on by their individual actions. Without a seed there would be no fruit; without action, the six realms would not exist. The seed of karma is planted by our minds. It flowers when body, speech, and mind carry out the actions and it bears fruit in the effects we experience later in our lives. There are six ways for us to look at karma, beginning with its divisions and characteristics. The remaining four concern the qualities of karma: Each individual will experience the results of their own actions; each action has a direct result; the results of each action are endless; and the results of each action will not disappear though they may be balanced by an opposite action.

There are three divisions of karma: unwholesome, wholesome, and immoveable. Unwholesome actions are negative ones, wholesome actions are positive ones, and immoveable ones are those which are undiluted by conflicting emotions. Immoveable actions are unusual and have very powerful virtuous effect.

The characteristics of karma vary depending on which division we are viewing. There are Ten Nonvirtuous Actions which constitute the unwholesome division of karma. Each action is the cause of a clear effect. The three bodily nonvirtuous actions are killing, stealing, and sexual misconduct.

The act of killing may be motivated by desire, anger, or ignorance. To kill for the sake of gain is to kill from desire; to kill out of hatred is to kill from anger; and to kill thinking there is virtue in it is to kill from ignorance. An example of killing for gain would be killing an animal for its flesh. An example of killing from anger would be killing someone we hate. An example of killing from ignorance would be killing for the purpose of blood sacrifice or offering flesh to deities in the belief that those acts might bring protection from suffering or benefit and happiness. The result of killing is to be reborn in the hell realms where beings are endlessly murdered; to be reborn as a human with a short and unhealthy life; or to be reborn in an unfortunate land.

The second bodily nonvirtuous act is stealing. There are three forms: stealing by strength, as when we overpower someone and take their possessions; stealing by skill, as when we take something and the owner does not know it; and stealing by deception, as when we sell something we do not own. The result of stealing is to be reborn in the hungry ghost realm where beings are always in need; to be reborn as a human in great poverty; or to be reborn in a land of little food and poor harvests.

The third bodily nonvirtuous act is sexual misconduct. Sexual misconduct by relationship means that it is nonvirtuous for us to have intercourse with blood relatives. Sexual misconduct by honor means that we should not have intercourse with anyone who is pledged or committed to another. Sexual misconduct by religious reasons is described in five ways: "imperfect organ" prohibits anal and oral intercourse; "imperfect place" prohibits intercourse in shrines or other holy areas; "imperfect time" prohibits intercourse during times when one has vowed to abstain and during naturally unsuitable times such as pregnancy or illness; "imperfect limit" prohibits intercourse more than five times daily; and "imperfect method" prohibits intercourse based on violence. The result of sexual misconduct is to be reborn in the hungry ghost realms where desire is never satisfied; to be reborn as a human whose spouse has many enemies; or to be reborn in a dusty land.

The four nonvirtuous actions involving the speech are lying, slander, harsh talk, and meaningless talk. Lying occurs if spiritual achievements are exaggerated, if the truth is altered to help oneself and harm others, or if the truth is altered just to amuse the speaker. The result of lying is to be reborn in the animal realm where beings cannot know right from wrong; to be reborn as a human who is irresponsible and unrespected; or to be reborn as a human who has sour breath.

Slander involves creating trouble between two friends who are face to face, seducing friends away from a person behind their back, and spreading untrue stories through a third party. The result of slander is to be reborn in the hell realms where loyalty is unknown; to be reborn as a friend-less human; or to be reborn in a rocky land.

Harsh talk includes saying mean and unpleasant things directly to people, hiding nasty opinions in jokes or other apparently harmless talk, or spreading malicious opinions behind a person's back. The result is to be reborn in the hungry ghost realms where gentleness does not exist; to be reborn a human who hears and is frightened by unpleasant sounds; or to be reborn in a dry, harsh land.

Meaningless talk encompasses recitation of mantra in-correctly and recitation of black magic spells with the goal of harming another; nonsensical or pointless talk; and shar-ing the Dharma with someone who is uninterested. The result of meaningless talk is to be reborn in the animal realms where there is no meaningful communication; to be reborn as a human who cannot grasp the meaning of things; or to be reborn in a land where seasons are often reversed or confused.

The three nonvirtuous actions involving the mind are en-vy, ill will, and wrong views. Envy arises if we are jealous for ourselves, that is, full of pride and attachment; if we are covetous of others' qualities or accomplishments, or if we are covetous of material things. The result of envy is to be reborn in the hungry ghost realms where each being envies what they cannot possess; to be reborn a human with a huge ego that is never satisfied; or to be reborn in a land of poor harvests.

Ill will is motivated by anger toward others, by jealous desire of their possessions, and by seeking revenge for old wrongs. The result of ill will is to be reborn in the hell realms where good will is unknown; to be reborn a human who is angry; or to be reborn in an unpleasant land which serves hot and bitter foods.

Wrong views arise if we refuse to believe in the results of cause and effect, if we refuse to believe in the power of the Dharma to pacify emotions and attain liberation, and if we refuse to believe in the teacher Buddha, his teachings of the Dharma, and its followers in the Sangha. The result of these actions is to be reborn in the animal realms where stupidity prevail; to be reborn a human who is too stupid to understand any high teaching, especially the Dharma; or to be reborn in a land of poverty.

There are some common features among the Ten Nonvirtous Actions which constitute the unwholesome division of karma. First, any nonvirtuous action has a greater significance and therefore a greater result if it is directed toward one's parents, one's guru, enlightened beings, or practitioners of the Dharma. Second, the general result of angry actions is the hell realms, the general result of actions motivated by desire is the hungry ghost realms, and the general result of stupid actions is the animal realms. Third, when the number of nonvirtuous actions is considered, a large quantity leads to the hell realms, a medium number leads to the hungry ghost realm, and a small number to the animal realm. When judged by the objects, nonvirtuous actions directed toward special objects, such as Buddhas, bodhisattvas, and teachers lead to the hell realms. Actions directed toward moderate objects lead to the hungry ghost realms and those directed toward ordinary objects lead to the animal realms.

The second division of karma is wholesome deeds. The characteristics of this division are seen in the Ten Virtuous Actions, which are the opposite of the actions described above. The three virtuous bodily actions are saving lives, giving possessions to others, and behaving properly sexually. Saving lives results in rebirth either as a god, as a human who has long life and many comforts, or as a human in a pleasant land. Being generous with possessions leads either

to rebirth as a ruler, as a human with wealth and possessions, or in a land of plenty. Conducting ourselves sexually
in the proper way leads to rebirth as a god, as a human
whose marriage and friendships are full of harmony, or in
a comfortable land.

The four virtuous actions of speech are speaking the
truth, mediating disputes, speaking kindly, and speaking
meaningfully. Speaking the truth results in rebirth as a
human who is highly regarded as honest and lives in a level
land of rich harvests. Mediating disputes leads to rebirth as
a god or a human who is reliable and lives in a land of fair
weather. Speaking kindly results in rebirth as a god or
human who is praised by all and lives in a temperate land.
Speaking meaningfully leads to rebirth as a human who is
happy to speak little and lives in a land of even geography
and temperature.

The three virtuous activities of the mind are being content, having compassion and having faith. Being content
leads to rebirth as a god or a human who is happy and lives
in a pleasant land. Having good will and compassion results
in life as a god or a human who is loved and lives in a land
where needs are filled. Having faith leads to rebirth as a god
or a human of great intelligence who lives in a fertile land.

The third division of karma is immoveable actions. These
actions are concerned with developing samadhi at ever-
increasing levels and include virtuous actions which are
free from conflicting emotions. The result of immoveable actions is rebirth in the god realm, proceeding from first level
samadhi god through formless god to nonperception god.
The limitation of immoveable actions is seen particularly at
this highest level for, while being beyond perception is an
achievement, it is also the end to motivation for action and is
the seed of its own destruction. The god at this level lives a
life of pleasure and without continued virtuous actions, that
life will end. Even the gods are caught in samsara because the

samadhi which is sought in immoveable actions is worldly samadhi rather than spiritually-enlightened samadhi.

There are four remaining facts about karma. First, whatever actions we do will affect only ourselves. Neither virtuous nor nonvirtuous actions can be given away or passed to any other being or inanimate object. Second, virtuous actions lead to happy results and nonvirtuous actions lead to unhappy results. For us to expect good things to come of mean actions is rather like expecting an orange to grow on an apple tree.

Third, each small action has an inexhaustible effect. The Buddha said that one harsh word can cause five hundred years of suffering and one virtuous thought purifies an eon. The analogy of planting an apple seed may be expanded here. If we do one virtuous act in planting the seed, and if we water and fertilize it by continuing to do virtuous actions, a tree will grow from which will come thousands of apples, that is, thousands of happy results.

Fourth, karma can never be exhausted, though it can be balanced by actions of the opposite nature. If we are seeing the fruits of harmful actions, we must accept that these will not disappear. We can, however, begin to redress the balance by acting beneficially, and we must accept that this karma will not disappear, either.

After this discussion it is easy to see the importance of turning our efforts toward virtuous actions. The body is like a horse and the mind is like a rider. It is the rider's right and responsibility to choose the direction of the journey. If the rider chooses the path of least resistance, the journey may be easy but the horse and rider may not arrive at their destination. To take the journey toward final happiness, the mind must lead the body through many dangers and much hard work.

In America, much of the raw material for this journey out of samsara is available. You are free to practice the religion of your choice and you have many kinds of work and life-style available to you. It is possible for many people to live comfortable happy lives here and be free from want. What this means is that it should be easier to turn your attention to the implications of karma and to direct the body, speech, and mind toward wholesome deeds. It is the law of karma which finally empowers our understanding of the faults of samsara and impermanence, and motivates us to take full advantage of our precious human existence. Let us not waste this life!

Questions

You say that killing is one of the ten nonvirtuous actions. What importance is it if we kill someone or something accidentally? Like a bug, for instance.

Mistaken or unknowing acts have their own results (karma), but it is not as strong as the karma that arises from knowing acts. This is true of both virtuous and nonvirtuous acts. Killing something accidentally is considered "unknowing killing" and can be purified by doing some daily purification, such as the Seven Branch Prayer, or by repeating the mantra "Om Mani Peme Hung" which transmutes the six poisons into the six wisdoms.

What about the state of being in between life and death? Being in a coma is just like being dead in some ways. Is the person still there if their personality is gone or dormant?

It is just as if they were asleep. The person is definitely still there until physical death occurs. That is why it is so important that you not terminate someone's life in that coma. Their karma includes that coma. You should do what you can to bring them back to life and then it is up to them. Even if they are in a coma, they are alive.

Why do sentient beings give birth if they know what great suffering lies ahead for their young?

It is the parents' karma to give birth and the child's karma to be born to those parents. There is no choice, really. By the time conception happens, the choices were made by the karma of parents' and child's actions in their present and past lives.

We can't avoid suffering by trying not to be born. The only way out of the cycle of rebirth is to go beyond it by becoming enlightened. The enlightened beings are the only ones who have any choice about being born, and they have complete freedom to be born or not to be born. They can choose the time and place and parents that will benefit beings the most. This is the state of freedom we all long for.

Does the increase in human population mean that more beings are drawing closer to enlightenment?

No. Unfortunately, most of the increases in human populations are in places and conditions of the world where human life is just as difficult and painful as in the lower realms. The precious human existence is still quite rare and you must remember that even if it became quite common, that humans would still be outnumbered many times over by the beings in the animal realm and other realms.

Is it better to help others or to meditate for others?

It is best to do both if we are able and if it is appropriate. However, meditation can help more beings at any given moment, if it is done with the proper motivation.

Chapter Two
Objects of Refuge

The main practice of the great Mahasiddha Atisha was the recitation of refuge prayers. When he came to Tibet from India in the eleventh century A.D., he taught the Tibetan people about refuge by explaining and practicing it. Because of this the Tibetan people call him "The Refuge Lama." Atisha was not a beginner, and he was not an unknowledgable being. He was a great Bodhisattva and had completely realized all the teachings of Buddhism. Atisha had discovered that refuge is the essential teaching, the essential practice. He taught that the only practice one needs is refuge; it contains everything. It contains the Three Jewels of Buddha, Dharma, and Sangha, and the Three Roots of Lama, Yidam, and Dharma Protector; no other practice is needed.

Refuge is a profound and very advanced practice. Indeed, it is the most important part of Buddhism. Unfortunately, many people think of it as a beginner's practice and do not believe it is necessary even to have it explained. However, it is the important first step on the Buddhist path and the source of all other practices. Refuge is the foundation on which the Mahayana Bodhisattva Vow is built and the Bodhisattva Vow is the foundation for the Vajrayana vows. Then, step by step, come other practices. The greater and deeper the practices become, the more important and profound refuge becomes.

Many people think that taking refuge means belonging to some group and giving up independence. This is not true. In reality, when we take refuge, we give up only what is useless and destructive in ourselves.

What does it mean to take refuge? In a worldly sense, there may be many situations in which we seek protection. For example, when the land of Tibet was invaded and occupied by China in 1959, it was a very painful and bitter time. China tried to control the culture and religion. Parents were separated from children and husbands from wives. People lost control over their own lives and needed a refuge to escape from these problems.

The difficulty facing the people of Tibet was to find some place that could offer sanctuary. Their neighbor India was a large country that had the power and resources to protect and aid them. When asked to help, the Indians responded generously. Many Tibetans escaped to India where the Chinese were unable to follow.

In a spiritual sense, refuge is not only for the Tibetan people, but for all sentient beings, that is, all beings with consciousness. All beings have an enemy in the conflicting emotions that destroy their comforts, pleasures, and freedoms. The chief foe, ignorance, leads all the others: desire, anger, pride, jealousy, and greed. These are our permanent adversaries because they deceive us, injuring our permanent happiness, our permanent freedom. They oppress the true nature of our mind which is intrinsically free from conflicting emotions and obscurations.

We have been in this world numberless times and have not been able to escape from the cycle of existence. We have tried many ways to escape to freedom and happiness. We may hope to do this on our own but we cannot succeed. We don't have the power to stand against the habit of conflicting emotions and we don't have help from anyone. This is when we need refuge.

The habit of conflicting emotion is the most dangerous enemy of all because it follows us from life to life. Children who have just been born already know how to cry, how to express anger and happiness. No one taught them this. The child has changed the physical form but has not changed the habits which are brought into being by past actions and continue with the mind from life to life. Therefore, sometimes we are sick, sometimes healthy, sometimes happy, and sometimes unhappy; this reflects the actions of the past.

When we die, who is it who is reborn? Suppose we go to sleep and dream of some other place such as India. There we travel about, eat, enjoy friendship, and have lots of happy and unhappy experiences. Who is in the dream? Our existence is a dream, and life after life the dreamer is the one who will be born, who will suffer, and feel the results of all previous actions. In order to break this cycle of existence, we have to break our habits by practicing pure habits and avoiding impure ones. When we first try to practice beneficial habits, we see that the effort does not last very long because harmful habits are more powerful. We need some kind of refuge, someone who can lead us in the right direction towards escape from confusion and suffering.

We need a special object of refuge for protection. This cannot be found in the world of conflicting emotions so we turn to Buddha Shakyamuni who is the object of refuge. Why do we take refuge in him? What kind of qualifications does he have to protect us from these enemies?

In Tibetan, the Buddha is called "Sanggye."* "Sang" means "clear weather without any clouds." The Buddha

---

*Editor's Note: In this text, all Tibetan terms are spelled as they are pronounced. For orthographic spelling and further information, refer to the Glossary.

has completely purified conflicting emotions so his mind is free from suffering and calm like clear weather. "Gye" means "to increase or flourish." Other Tibetan names for the Buddha are "Ku Shi," meaning "Four Bodies," and "Yeshe Nga" meaning "Five Wisdoms." These two names refer to qualities of the Buddha in which we can take refuge.

The first of the Four Bodies ("Ku Shi") is the Svabhavikakaya (Tib: Ngowonyi Kyi Ku) or the essential body. It is the unity of the remaining three bodies. The second body, the Dharmakaya (Tib: Chö Kyi Ku) is emptiness and permeates all things. Because it is beyond the realm of intellect, it cannot be seen. Dharmakaya is pure mind. The third body is called the Sambhogakaya (Tib: Longcho Zog Ku). It is the enjoyment body, and the fields where it is enjoyed are the pure Buddha realms. Sambhogakaya is pure speech. The fourth body is called the Nirmanakaya (Tib: Trülpai Ku), the emanation body, and it appears in different forms according to the needs of sentient beings. Nirmanakaya is pure physical body, pure action. The Buddha Shakyamuni, Guru Padmasambhava, and other high incarnation lamas are seen in the Nirmanakaya. From beginningless time, the emanation body appears in physical form to liberate sentient beings according to their needs. These beings effortlessly and spontaneously manifest out of their compassion.

These Four Bodies represent the qualities of the Buddha. The bodies are not separate from each other nor do they act separately. The Svabhavikakaya is the essential body since the essential act is to be completely free from obscurations. The Svabhavikakaya represents the unity of the three remaining bodies (also called the "three kayas"). The Buddha has completely cleared away the conflicting emotions and as a result, he is completely pure. Only such a being can give refuge.

The Buddha also has Five Wisdoms ("Yeshe Nga") instead of our five mind poisons of ignorance, anger, pride, desire, and jealousy. The first wisdom is that of the Dharmadhatu (Tib: Chökyi Ching Kyi Yeshe), endless sphere of the dharma, which is completely indestructible. This wisdom is ignorance purified.

The second wisdom is called Mirror-like Wisdom (Tib: Meelong Yeshe) and it is omniscient because its clarity is not obstructed or obscured. When you polish a mirror, anything you put in front of it will be reflected without obscuration. When the Buddha wants to benefit beings, distance does not matter; he is able to see clearly without any obscurations or obstructions. This wisdom is anger purified.

The third wisdom is the Wisdom of Equanimity (Tib: Nyampanyi Yeshe). Buddha is not obstructed by hatred or desire. He is like a close friend rather than an enemy. His wisdom has no resistance or acceptance; it sees all and is given equally to all sentient beings. This wisdom is pride purified.

The fourth wisdom is the Wisdom of Discrimination (Tib: Soso Tokpai Yehse). This means that his wisdom is not mixed with ignorance. When we learn something, we may be mistaken. The Buddha's discriminating wisdom, however, enables him to see all individual beings and their actions and karma, what they have done in the past, what they are doing now, and what they will do in the future. This wisdom is desire purified.

The fifth wisdom is called the All-accomplishing Wisdom (Tib: Chapa Tubyai Yeshe). This means that all beings are benefited by Buddha's activity and he does not need to make preparations or think about how he will accomplish their benefit. This wisdom is jealousy purified.

Ordinary beings do not have these Five Wisdoms and the activity of the Four Bodies, so it would be foolish to make an ordinary being the object of our refuge. Only the Buddha, who has completely removed the five poisons, is completely pure and qualified to give us refuge. His infinite wisdom is joined with skillful means so that he is able to protect us and lead us from samsara (Tib: Khorwa). The Buddha is the first object of refuge, the first of the Three Jewels.

The next object of refuge, the second of the Three Jewels, is the jewel-like Dharma. There is a Dharma of Precept and a Dharma of Realization. The Dharma of Precept consists of the scriptures, the teachings of the Buddha, which in Sanskrit are called "sutras." There are 84,000 of these, divided into three main groups, the Vinaya, the Bodhisatvayana, and the Abidharma. Together, these three groups of sutras are called Tripitaka.

The Vinaya sutras concern moral discipline and are the antidote of desire. The Bodhisatvayana sutras, such as the Lotus Sutra, concern love and compassion. They are the antidote of anger and also reduce selfishness through their concern with other sentient beings. The Abhidharma is the antidote of ignorance and contains the Prajna Paramita, the perfection of wisdom.

The Dharma of Realization is seen when practicing the truth of separation, a process whereby we pacify our conflicting emotions and differentiate them from the true nature of our minds. As we read the scriptures and hear the teachings, our thinking is refined and doubt and hesitation are destroyed. We do the practices and learn to separate emotions from the nature of the mind. Then we can develop wisdom, the "truth of the path," and this is the Dharma of Realization.

Realization is not like being educated to be a doctor. That education will provide us with respectability and a good living, but after we die, the education will be of no use in the next life. However, if we are diligent enough to practice these dharmas, the wisdom obtained will become a habit and will be of permanent help. From this practice we can receive the joy of bliss which we call freedom. This precious and rare object of refuge we call the Second Jewel—the Dharma Jewel.

The Third Jewel is the Sangha. This can refer to the monastic order and also to anyone who dedicates his or her life to the liberation of all sentient beings. Sangha can also mean the glorious assembly of tenth-level Bodhisattvas. These are beings who have deep realization of the Prajna Paramita of emptiness and wisdom. Out of this realization comes objectless and effortless compassion for all sentient beings.

So the Three Jewels in which we can take refuge are, first, the Buddha, an ordinary person who attained a completely transformative awakening; second, the Dharma, a practice which transforms our impurities and develops our wisdom; and third, the Sangha, the dedicated people and great Bodhisattvas who support our efforts to reach enlightenment.

When we become realized, we will no longer need the Sangha or the Dharma; the Buddha alone will be our object of refuge. Now, however, the Buddha's attainment is far above us; to reach his level of realization we need the Dharma and Sangha. At this time they are more necessary than the Buddha to guide us upon the path to enlightenment.

If we compare existence to an ocean of suffering, then the Dharma is a boat and the Sangha is the captain who navigates the boat to the farther shore where the Buddha is. A boat without a captain's guidance is a vessel going nowhere. A captain without a boat will accomplish very little, since it is not possible to carry all the passengers on the captain's back. Likewise we need both the vehicle of the Dharma to hold us on our journey and the experienced guidance of the Sangha to see us through to enlightenment.

When we arrive at the farther shore of enlightenment, we won't need to carry the boat with us and we will no longer need the captain; when we reach the Buddha, we will no longer need the Dharma or the Sangha. The only object of refuge will be the Buddha, because we are the Buddha. We will have become the object of refuge itself.

It is important to state that these descriptions of the Three Jewels come from the Mahayana tradition of Buddhism. Mahayana means "great vehicle." The followers of the "lesser vehicle," the Hinayana, take refuge in the Buddha alone, and pledge themselves to work from now until death to liberate themselves from samsaric suffering. Hinayana Dharma is based on the Vinaya sutras alone and concerns the pacification of emotions.

The Hinayana Sangha strives to attain Arhatship—the word Arhat meaning "pure destroyer." This title refers to the fact that those who have achieved this level have destroyed their conflicting emotions and no longer have any attachment to samsara. This Sangha consists of two types of practitioners. First, there are the Shravakas (Tib: Nyabthu) or "listeners" who follow only the self-liberation teachings, are very disgusted by the samsaric world and are seemingly afraid to benefit sentient beings. Secondly, there are the Pratyeka Buddhas (Tib: Rang Sanggye) or "self-Buddhas" who wish to free themselves from samsara but avoid aiding or liberating others for fear of being stained by emotion. They are very isolated from other beings as they seek freedom from suffering.

The Mahayana way to take refuge in the Three Jewels is first to visualize that all sentient beings without exception have gathered with us to take refuge. We and numberless beings are taking refuge in numberless Buddhas and Bodhisattvas abiding in numberless pure lands. With devotion to the purity and wisdom of the Three Jewels, we offer our speech, mind, body, whatever material wealth we have, and all things of value that exist in this world, to the objects of refuge. When we make this offering, we do not give up anything or give away anything. Taking refuge means that we completely devote our lives to the Three Jewels. If we are diligent about this commitment, refuge will eliminate our problems. If troubles persist, we must examine our devotion and diligence to find what is inadequate in our practice of taking refuge.

In the tradition of the Vajrayana, the "diamond-like vehicle," a person takes refuge not only in the Three Jewels but also in the Three Roots of Lama, Yidam, and Dharma Protector. The Lama is the embodiment of the Three Jewels. The mind of the Lama is seen to be the Buddha, the Lama's speech is the Dharma, and the Lama's body is the Sangha.

The Lama is known as the Blessing Root, embodying and maintaining the blessings of the Buddha which have been passed from teacher to student in an unbroken lineage from Buddha Shakyamuni to the present guru. For the Vajrayana student, the Lama becomes the primary Refuge. Since we don't hear or see the Buddha ourselves, it is the Lama who transmits the blessings directly to us.

There are three ways that the Lama transmits the blessings: by teaching, by symbol, and by action. The first and most ordinary way to give transmission is through teaching. The guru teaches us to understand the necessity of avoiding nonvirtuous activities and engaging in virtuous ones. The Lama also teaches us to generate the enlightened attitude, instructs us in form and formless meditation and introduces us to our wisdom mind.

The second way that the blessings are transmitted is by symbol. This is done through the Lama giving initiations or empowerments, using ritual objects. The Lama gives us blessings by allowing us to experience these initiations and by teaching us about the symbols and their meaning.

The third way to transmit blessings is through actions. At these times the Lama will not be giving a formal teaching or using ritual symbols, but will be engaged in seemingly ordinary activity which is the means of transmitting the blessing. For example, the guru Marpa instructed his student Milarepa to build houses and then tear them down again. He did not give Milarepa any dharma teachings or initiations but instructed him instead to work almost beyond the limits of his physical endurance. Although to many, Marpa's actions might have seemed nonsensical or cruel, Milarepa had no doubts about his teacher and knew that Marpa could purify his negative karma. Today we could never believe that building a house would lead to enlightenment, but Milarepa did achieve it. After working for Marpa and receiving his blessings, Milarepa was able, through his devotion, to cut off his samsaric attachment. He was in mountain retreat for twelve years and achieved enlightenment during that time. Marpa's extraordinary actions were deeper teachings than any Milarepa could have found in texts or initiations.

Another example of blessings transmitted by the Lama's actions is found in this story of the student Asangha who was very devoted to the Buddha Maitreya and hoped to see him and take teachings from him. At the time, Maitreya was one of the eight heart-son disciples of the Buddha. In pursuit of the teachings, Asangha spent some time meditating in isolated retreat but was unable to see Maitreya. Disheartened, he left his retreat and came upon what appeared to be a poor man, but was actually Maitreya in disguise. This man's home was located near a stream overshadowed by a rock and Asangha found him throwing handfuls of water at the rock. When Asangha asked him what he was doing, the man explained that because of the position of the rock, his house received no sunlight; by throwing water on the rock, he intended to wear it away. Asangha was astounded and said that it could take years or even many lifetimes, and the man said, "If you are diligent enough, you can succeed at anything you want. You have to be diligent." Asangha was deeply touched and realized that if this man could be so dedicated to a worldly goal, he could surely return to retreat for his spiritual goal.

Asangha returned to his cave, but by the end of three years he again became discouraged at not being able to see Maitreya and left his retreat. Once again he met Maitreya, this time disguised as a man holding a long, thick piece of iron. He was gently rubbing the iron with a soft woolen cloth. When Asangha asked him what he was doing, he said, "I am exhausting the iron to make a needle to sew clothes." Once again Asangha was inspired to match this man's diligence and he returned to retreat.

After nine years, Asangha had still been unable to see Maitreya and he left his cave. He met a female dog who had many festering sores and wounds. She was screaming in agony and Asangha could see maggots in the wounds. He saw this as his opportunity to help beings, so he tried to think of the best way to be of help. If he pulled the maggots out, they would die and he would be responsible for killing them. If he didn't remove them, the dog would die and his inaction would have killed her; he also would have lost his opportunity to help. He tried to think of a gentle way to remove the maggots without harming them and realized that his tongue was the softest part of his body. He decided to gently lick the wounds, thus removing the maggots safely, and dedicated his actions to benefit all beings. He closed his eyes and knelt down to lick one of the wounds and was astonished when his tongue touched the ground. He looked up to see that the dog was gone and Maitreya was standing there instead. He was overjoyed and prostrated himself to Maitreya.

Maitreya said, "I have been above your head for all these years, but because of your impurities, you could not see me. Your goal, to see me for yourself alone, was a selfish one. But when you had compassion for this dog, and through her, for all beings, your pure motive enabled you to see me. If you don't believe that I was near you and you just were unable to see me, carry me into town on your shoulders and observe the responses of the townspeople."

Asangha did carry Maitreya through the town and asked the townspeople if they saw what he carried on his shoulders. Except for one old woman who said he carried a dead dog, everyone said he carried nothing at all. They thought he was crazy.

So the Lama is the Blessing Root, the one who receives the blessing from the lineage and passes it on to the disciples. The Lama can give us the seed but not the fruit; the Lama can give us the blessing but not the accomplishments.

The Yidams are the personal deities which accomplish realization. They are known as the Accomplishment Root. We must utilize the teachings, initiations, and actions of the Lama in order to visualize the deities and make our body, speech, and mind inseparable from the deities' body, speech, and mind. Our body becomes the deities' body, our speech becomes the deities' mantra, and our mind becomes the mind of the deities. The true nature of the deities is emptiness. All the deities are the wisdom of the Buddha, appearing out of compassion and manifesting, according to the needs of beings, in many wrathful and peaceful forms. Becoming inseparable from the deities purifies the obstacles of our body, speech, and mind and leads to our accomplishment.

The Dharma Protectors are the Activity Root. When we practice the purification of body, speech, and mind, our habitual tendencies arise with greater power to make us miserable. The Dharmapalas or Dharma Protectors act externally to cut off these obstacles on the path. They protect us from misdirection caused by ourselves or others and lead us in the right direction.

From the tantric perspective, the Three Roots are the main refuge. Without the proper understanding, it might appear that the Three Roots are separate from the Three Jewels but we must realize that the mind of the Lama is Buddha, the speech of the Lama is the Dharma, and the body of the Lama is the Sangha. It is the guru who is present to lead us to enlightenment. As we proceed further into the practice, we realize that the Lama's body is the Dharma Protectors, the Lama's speech is the Yidams, and the Lama's mind is the Lama itself. So all Three Jewels and all Three Roots are contained within the Lama. When we have truly deepened our practice, we merge our mind with the Lama's mind and we become our own refuge.

Questions

From whom do we take the refuge vow?

The Lama is the source of the refuge vow, the person we trust to explain it and give it to us. The more we believe in the Lama and the more motivated we are to take refuge, the more powerful the experience will be.

You say that the Lama's mind is Buddha. Is that because of the lineage back to Shakyamuni Buddha?

Well, actually the Lama's mind is supposed to be Buddha because it is free from obscuration. "La" means "above." All sentient beings' minds are under the sway of the five poisons; Buddha-mind has overcome these poisons and therefore is "above" them. "Ma" means "mother." What is meant here is that this is a person who has purity, wisdom, and great compassion for all beings, just as a mother has for her child. Great wisdom and great compassion are the outstanding qualities of the Lama.

What are the strengths and weaknesses of the Hinayana practice?

One strong point of Hinayana practice is the discipline and desire to root out all conflicting emotion. The Hinayana Buddhists think the sufferings of samsara are really disgusting and they want to get to nirvana, the state of cessation. The discipline and desire to achieve this can lead to great purification. But this great motivation can also be a weakness in the Hinayana practice because they do it only for themselves. They destroy external phenomena but are still ruled by their selfishness.

Are there differences in the meditation practices of the Hinayana and Mahayana?

No, the meditation practices do not generally differ. Developing concentration requires similar methods. The two schools utilize breath, recitation, and mantra. However, the Hinayana school does not visualize deities.

What is the difference between karma and habit?

Karma is what you suffer now; habit is what creates your future karma. For example, I might have a habit of going fishing. That habit would bring me to the river and lead me to the action of fishing. When I catch a fish and it dies, I have the karma and will see results from it in this or other lives. The reason we should struggle to do good is because it can become a habit, too, with beneficial karma coming to us in this and future lives.

Are the things which happen in our dreams a reflection of our karma?

No, they are a reflection of habit. Sometimes you will dream of what you said or thought or did during the day or even during another lifetime.

The motive for taking refuge is to escape samsara and attain Buddhahood for the benefit of all beings. I can relate to escaping samsara but Buddhahood seems pretty far away. How can I develop aspiration and diligence?

Aspiration grows as you realize why you want to achieve something. If you can relate to escaping samsara, then think about all the beings who will be left behind if you succeed alone. If you can aspire to help beings in their worldly suffering, imagine how much more your efforts toward enlightenment will help them. If you truly understand the benefits of your practice, you will aspire to do it more.

Diligence comes from the "four thoughts which turn the mind"—the Four Foundations. If you understand the gift of the precious human body and the suffering that comes from impermanence, samsara, and karma, then you will naturally be diligent. The foundation practices make you diligent; the more you practice, the more diligent you become.

Some spiritual teachers say, "Just leave everything and go meditate." If we really did this, how would we live?

Very few people can leave everything and meditate. You should practice being skillful. Go to work and support yourself as people do in this society. Then, instead of spending all evening watching television, do your practice. It is important to take care of your responsibilities and also to practice. You do not have to give up one to do the other.

But can we reach enlightenment soon if we don't renounce the world?

If you have high motivation and diligence and devotion, that is what counts. If you renounce everything and don't have high motivation and diligence and devotion, that act of renunciation is meaningless. Someday in this country it may be possible to be supported in retreat, but until that day you must support yourself and pursue your practice. Renouncing everything doesn't make you enlightened. Practice makes you enlightened.

Chapter Three
Guru-Disciple Relationship

The guru-disciple relationship is a difficult one for Westerners to understand. There are many teachers in this world, from school teachers to people who teach us some skill. But for the Mahayana and Vajrayana student, the relationship with the teacher, the guru, is different from any other relationship we will have. In these traditions the teacher is called our "spiritual friend" without whom we cannot hope to become free from suffering or attain Buddhahood.

The first thing needed to reach enlightenment is Buddha nature. In other words, we must have a mind. Trees and stones cannot get enlightened because they do not have a mind and do not produce any karma. The mind is the seed of enlightenment.

Next, we must have favorable conditions. These include human existence, which is very difficult to obtain as it requires a great accumulation of virtue. Another favorable condition is understanding the importance of a spiritual practice. Many of us attain human existence but our minds are just like animals in that they lack the awareness of the need for a spiritual practice. It is rare to understand its importance.

Even if we have the favorable conditions, however, our negative habitual tendencies stand in the way of our attaining enlightenment. We need a teacher to awaken us to these tendencies and direct us on the path to Buddhahood.

We can look at the importance of meeting the spiritual friend in five ways: reasons for meeting the spiritual friend, categories, characteristics, skillful means needed by the student to establish a connection with the spiritual friend, and the benefits of that meeting.

There are three reasons for meeting a teacher. The first reason is cited in the sutras. Buddha said we should venerate and practice under a wise guru because it is from the guru that we receive good qualities.

The second reason for meeting a teacher is that this person is essential to us. To reach full enlightenment we must accumulate wisdom and merit, and since we don't know how to do this, we need the guidance of a teacher. Also we must learn to avoid the two obscurations of karma and not-knowing, and again, the guru gives us this instruction. The Buddhas all found it essential to study under a teacher in order to gain understanding of the path, to gain experience of the path, and to have full realization of the path.

The third reason for meeting a spiritual friend may be seen in a few examples. Imagine that we are walking alone on an unfamiliar path. It is easy to make mistakes in direction and to get lost or discouraged. However, if we have a guide who knows the path, we will feel confident and quickly accomplish our journey. Likewise when we are alone on the unfamiliar path to enlightenment, we may get confused, lost or discouraged; if we meet a teacher who knows the way, we will quickly and assuredly finish our journey to Buddhahood.

Imagine now that we are risking our lives and possessions to make a dangerous but necessary journey. If we travel alone, we may become victims of thieves who wish to take our wealth or of murderers who wish to take our lives; if we could find a strong protector, we could take the journey in safety. When we travel the dangerous path to enlightenment alone, the thieves of conflicting emotions try to steal the wealth of our accumulated wisdom and merit. Outer dangers, such as demons produced by our own egos, try to kill the life force of our precious human existence. If we can find a strong protector in the spiritual teacher, we can take the journey to enlightenment in safety.

The final example is one in which we imagine needing to cross a river. If we have no experience steering a boat on this river, we will have a difficult time getting across. If, however, we can find an experienced captain, our journey will be swift and sure. When we try to cross the river of samsara in the boat of the dharma, we may not have much success due to our inexperience. If we can find a captain in the guru, our journey to enlightenment will be swift and sure.

The second way to look at the importance of meeting the spiritual friend is to explore the four categories of these teachers. The categories are ordinary, Bodhisattva, Nirmanakaya, and Sambhogakaya spiritual friends. Of these four, the ordinary teacher is the most important for us and the one that we will meet first. When we have learned from the ordinary teacher and have been practicing the accumulation of great virtues, then we will be able to meet the great Bodhisattva spiritual friend. When we have almost, but not completely, eliminated the impurities of our body, speech, and mind, then we can contact the Nirmanakaya teacher. When we ourselves come to the level of the Bodhisattva, then we are able to contact the Sambhogakaya guru.

However, we can never meet these exalted beings without the ordinary spiritual friend. This teacher is not only our guide for the practice which may help us attain contact with higher levels of teachers, but also meets us in our very ordinary pain and confusion. We cannot expect to receive aid from the exalted beings but our ordinary guru is available to us when we are in need.

It is our ordinary teacher who introduces us to the Dharma. We naturally start wondering about it and we practice a little bit. We gain a little experience and then we practice a little more. It is through the kindness and blessing of the teacher that we progress along the path to Buddhahood and we should never forget this benevolence.

A story is told about remembering the kindness of the guru. There was a man who was a good spiritual teacher though he had no wealth or fame. One day this teacher and his best student were at a gathering, and another very famous guru was there. Formerly the student had prostrated himself to his teacher as a sign of respect, but that day he compared his guru to the famous one and was embarrassed by his teacher's poor appearance and obscure reputation. He hid from his teacher because he did not want to honor his teacher by prostrating himself.

Later that evening the student was doing his spiritual practice, which was a very high one due to the blessing of this teacher, and he had much confusion, fear, and doubt. He belatedly realized the benefits of his teacher and hurried the next day to prostrate himself. His teacher said he was not accepting this sign of respect since the student had obviously been filled with doubt the day before. The student asked how he could remove the doubt and regain his lost belief in the guru. He was told he must pray strongly and devotedly and stay alone in the mountains for twelve years.

It is all too easy for us to move from teacher to teacher or even to take just one teacher and then slowly forget to feel and show respect for them. It is said in the teachings of the Buddha that ignorance is darkness and our teacher is the light. Unfortunately, we may turn away from our teacher, as did the student in the story, before we realize the great value of light in our darkness. The ordinary spiritual friend is the one who brings us to the path of enlightenment and as such deserves our continued devotion and respect.

The third way to understand the importance of the spiritual friend is by looking at the characteristics of each category of teacher. Of course the Sambhogakaya and Nirmanakaya teachers are completely enlightened. They have abandoned all obscurations and are completely free of the poisons. These teachers are the manifestations of Dharmakaya, enlightenment itself, and are completely stainless and without fault.

The next category of spiritual friend is the Bodhisattva. In the *Bodhisattvabhumi*, Maitreya says that there are Ten Powers of the Bodhisattva. From the first level to the seventh level of the Bodhisattva path, the practitioner achieves the ordinary or external powers, and these are also the qualities of the ordinary spiritual friend; but from the eighth to the tenth level, the Bodhisattva achieves the Ten Special Powers. The first of these special powers is the Power of Life or Longevity, through which the Bodhisattvas are able to live as long as they wish. Second is the Mental Power, or Power of Concentration, through which they are able to concentrate without distraction. Third is the Power of Prosperity, through which they are able to bestow all that sentient beings desire, immeasurably providing for their needs.

Fourth is the Power of Karma, through which Bodhisattvas are able to transform sufferings resulting from negative karma to positive results through the means of exchanging, purifying, altering, and delaying these sufferings. Fifth is the Power of Rebirth, through which, while residing in deep concentration, the Bodhisattvas are able to be born in the various desire realms, yet remain unstained by any samsaric fault. Sixth is the Power of Aspiration, through which they are able to change or transform anything into whatever they wish. They can change water, earth, fire, or air into whatever they may require; they can fly in the sky and perform any other miraculous deeds they find necessary. Seventh is the Power of Dedication, through which they are able to immeasurably benefit themselves and others, and this dedication is assured to have the perfect result. Eighth is the Power of Miracles through which they are able to display miracles in order to discipline sentient beings.

The ninth special power is the Power of Wisdom, through which the Bodhisattvas become completely omniscient, certain of what must be abandoned and certain of all that is meaningful. Tenth is the Power of the Dharma, through which they are able to teach with language appropriate to each individual, completely satisfying the minds of others through the meanings of the various sutras.

The last category is ordinary spiritual friends and these have eight qualities. First they possess the Bodhisattva ethics and morals. Second, hearing the many sutras of the Bodhisattvas, they become learned and wise. Third, they achieve the realization of the Bodhisattva Path. Fourth, they are endowed with great mercy toward sentient beings. Fifth, they are endowed with fearlessness through which they do not recoil from the suffering of sentient beings nor do they fear helping sentient beings become free from their sufferings. Sixth, they are endowed with the strength of patience in the face of any hardship or difficulty. Seventh, they are free from hopelessness and do not regret or experience despair even in the most dire circumstances. Eighth, they are endowed with the meaning of the word. Their speech is meaningful, it achieves its result, and causes great benefit.

There are four other qualities mentioned by Maitreya. Hearing the sutras, the teachers acquire vast knowledge and understanding of the doctrine. They have great wisdom which cuts off the doubt of others. They perform the great activities of Superior Beings, so others can see that they are suitable to follow. Finally, they are endowed with the characteristic that purifies all the obscurations and misery.

Shantideva says in the *Bodhicharyvatara*:

Never, even at the cost of your life,
Should you forsake a spiritual friend
Who is wise in the meaning of the Great Vehicle
And who performs the supreme Bodhisattva Activities.

There are three skillful ways in which the student can establish a connection with the spiritual friend. First we must venerate and honor them, second we must have yearning and devotion for them, and third we must practice diligently.

To venerate our teacher means that we pay homage and show reverence. When we see our teacher, we need to be respectful in our bodily actions by bowing or making prostrations. We should be respectful in our speech by speaking from our heart in a very sweet and gentle manner. We can further honor our guru by making offerings of food and other material possessions.

The second skillful method of the student is to feel yearning and devotion toward the teacher. To do this, we must first see the guru as an enlightened being; then we can receive the blessings of an enlightened being. If we see the spiritual friend as an ordinary person, we will only receive the blessings of an ordinary person. If we forget our teacher's training and accomplishments, we may slide into doubts and disrespect, and lose our guide to enlightenment. However, if we can remember that the guru is Buddha himself, we can easily learn from the guru and do what is asked of us, trusting in the teacher's wisdom.

When our guru tells us to do something, we should do it without hesitation. There is a story told about Naropa who was a student of Tilopa. He was given twelve difficult tasks by his guru in order to earn the teachings and he tried to accomplish them all without doubt, hesitation, or wrong views. One of the tasks given to Naropa by his teacher was the instruction to marry. Now Naropa was a monk and, as such, was prohibited from marrying, but he believed in his teacher implicitly, so he married a young woman and lived with her as a husband should. Tilopa had told him that if he accomplished this task, he would give Naropa the Karma Yoga teachings, but after the marriage, Tilopa went into silent retreat for a year. Naropa viewed this disappointment philosophically, and even though his marriage was unhappy, he reasoned that he should remain married since his teacher had instructed him to do so.

When Tilopa ended his retreat he asked Naropa if he was well and then he asked why Naropa was married. "As a monk, you should know better. You must punish yourself." Naropa responded that it was not he who had made this mistake but his genitals. As punishment, he crushed his genitals between two rocks. Tilopa saw his devotion and gave him great blessings.

The next difficult task was when Tilopa asked Naropa to make him a gift of his wife. Naropa believed his teacher to be enlightened and did so without hesitation. When Naropa's wife, who resented being with an old man, tried to entice Naropa back, Tilopa beat her up.

In these times, it is difficult to conceive of such tasks and such devotion. Tilopa was not just taking advantage of Naropa and his wife, but was challenging their devotion and building their spiritual strength. This may seem a bit strange to us, but we must remember that this whole process of Tilopa teaching and testing Naropa with these twelve difficult tasks was one charged with magic and illusion, a supramundane reality. In each of Naropa's ordeals, he faced a situation which he could ultimately overcome only by recognizing his own delusion. In each case the situation was actually nothing more than a manifestation of the Guru Tilopa's skillful means. In this particular instance Naropa's wife was herself nothing other than a manifestation of Tilopa.

After Naropa had completed the twelve difficult tasks, he and Tilopa were walking in an arid place when Tilopa announced that he was finally ready to give the teachings. Naropa was to make the traditional offering preparations which included sprinkling water on the ground to keep the dust down, but there was no water in sight. Tilopa suggested that Naropa's blood would work as well as water and Naropa agreed. He slashed his body and the blood did indeed take care of the dust. His body also became his offering to the teacher; Tilopa, out of his compassion, struck Naropa on the head so he would be unconscious and not feel the pain of his act. Through Tilopa's blessing, Naropa awoke enlightened and saw Tilopa singing in the sky. "You are my son, now, and equal to your guru. Come join me." Naropa rose to the sky and realized that all the difficult tasks from his guru actually had been the teachings he had someday hoped to get.

It is vital that we learn from Naropa's example. When our teacher ignores us or asks difficult things of us, we must believe that these actions are the skillful means to purify us. A worldly teacher may treat us pleasantly, but we can only learn ordinary things from them. Our spiritual friend may treat us unpleasantly sometimes, but we can learn extraordinary things from them.

The third skillful method in building a strong connection with a spiritual friend is to practice diligently. The first step is to listen to our guru's teachings. Second, we must analyze the teachings to be sure we have heard and understood them correctly. Then we can put them into practice and develop our experience and realization. Of the three skillful methods available to the student, practice is the most pleasing to the spiritual friend.

Receiving teachings from our guru has three phases: preparation, taking the teachings, and conclusion. The preparation is done by developing the enlightened attitude, acknowledging that we will receive this teaching not only for self-liberation but also to help liberate all beings from suffering.

When we are taking the teachings, our attitude should be that we are ill, the teachings are the medicine, and the guru is the wise doctor. Our willingness to practice the teachings is viewed as the effort put forth to follow the doctor's prescription and take the medicine diligently to cure our illness.

The conclusion concerns our state of mind during the teachings and the results of having heard them. We should avoid having our mind be like an upside down cup, a cup with a hole in it, or a cup with poison in it. If we pour liquid on an upside down cup, it will wash over the cup and none of the liquid will be contained. If we take teachings with a mind which is somewhere else, the teachings will wash over us, and none of the teachings will be contained.

If we try to pour liquid into a cup with a hole in it, every drop will run right through. If our mind is not focused on the teaching, it will go in one ear and out the other and we will immediately forget what we have heard.

Finally, if we pour a delicious liquid into a cup with poison in it, the liquid will become poisoned. If our mind is full of the poisons of anger, jealousy, greed, etc., the teachings will be contaminated. We must work, then, to have our minds be attentive, focused, and clear of conflicting emotions in order to hear the teachings without distortion.

The last way for us to understand the importance of the spiritual friend is to examine the benefits of having one. The first benefit is that we will not be reborn in a lower realm after contact with a guru. We will be protected by the power of the teacher's speech and will be close to the Great Vehicle, the Mahayana, eventually reaching full enlightenment. The benefits we enjoy in this lifetime are a long, healthy, and happy life. The extraordinary benefit is that we will reach a state free from suffering and full of bliss and joy. We will be at the level of the Dharmakaya which is full enlightenment.

In conclusion, we must be very careful to keep the connection with the spiritual friend alive. This is particularly true in the Kagyu tradition which is built on the oral transmission from teacher to student. The great yogi Tilopa received his teachings from Vajradakini, a female wisdom dakini (Tib: Ka droma). Naropa was Tilopa's main student and he taught Marpa. Milarepa was Marpa's main student, and he taught Gompopa who taught the first Karmapa. The teachings have continued to be passed from guru to student ever since. Each of these teachers required their students to undergo tremendous trials. In this age, we are given easier tasks, such as the Ngöndro practice, but we can still receive the same blessings if we approach and cement a relationship with our own spiritual friend based on conviction, respect, and devotion.

Questions

I live far from my spiritual teacher. How can I build a close relationship?
The Lama's blessing has nothing to do with distance. You can receive it anywhere if you have devotion. Sometimes it is better to be at some distance from the guru. Because of our impurities, it is easy to take the teacher and the teachings for granted. If our time with the teacher is precious, we will value the relationship and the instruction more. In

Tibet, students might travel for many weeks to visit their Lama and get the answer to a single question. In America, you may be able to visit your Lama much more frequently, or to write or telephone. It is not the amount of time you spend with your Lama that counts, however, but what use you make of it.

How do we know which teacher we can be close to?

Finding a teacher doesn't mean you should run around looking for someone who is famous or friendly or wears certain clothing. It is your responsibility to listen to the teachers and analyze their words. If they speak the truth as far as you can tell, then it doesn't matter whether you like them or feel close to them. When we talk about student and teacher having a close connection, we are not talking about having a friendship! We are describing a relationship which ultimately will help you with your fears and doubts and conflicting emotions and lead you to enlightenment.

Is it true that an ordinary spiritual friend could also be a Bodhisattva?

Yes. If you have many impurities, you would see a regular person. As you became more pure, you would be able to see more. More purification leads to clearer perceptions.

Are the demonic forces you mentioned real?

The relative point of view is that there are real demons in our lives, as when someone is mad at us. The absolute point of view says that the demons are insubstantial, that they are external reflections of our ego-clinging.

It confuses me to think how hard I'm going to have to work to get enlightened when I don't even know what that means.

Here is a story that may help you. There was an old woman who lived in Tibet. Her son was a trader who often went to India and she asked him to bring her some relic of the Buddha Shakyamuni from his next trip. He agreed to do it but in all the hustle and hard work of the trip, he forgot.

This happened three times and finally the old woman told her son that if he didn't keep his word, she would kill herself in front of him.

He promised to fulfill her wish on his next trip but when he was halfway home, he realized he'd forgotten. He loved his mother and didn't want to disappoint her but it was too long a journey to think about turning around and going back to India. At this time he saw a dead dog in the road and thought it would solve his problem. He took one of the dog's teeth, polished it and wrapped it in cloth, and presented it to his mother as one of the Buddha's teeth.

The old woman was full of joy. She used the dog's tooth as her devotion object, having no idea that her son had lied to her. This woman had no teacher, but she had great devotion to the Buddha even though she had never met him or heard him teach. Her devotion was so focused that the tooth began to radiate light and rainbows and when the old woman died, she transformed into a rainbow too, which is a sign of great accomplishment.

Most of you are more fortunate than this old woman. You have dharma books to read and you can find a guru if you want; you will not be limited to a dog's tooth. But it is your desire for enlightenment and your devotion that are the most important part of your practice. This old woman didn't do her practice because she knew what the results would be; she did it because she felt devotion and wanted to express it.

Section II:
Aspirational and Operational Bodhi Mind

Chapter One
Aspirational Bodhi Mind

When we begin any spiritual practice, we must first examine our motivation. In order to practice the Mahayana Path, our motivation should not be for ourselves alone; we must seek to obtain Buddhahood for the sake of all living beings. Without this vast motivation, the practice becomes just another worldly activity.

In order to have this motivation we must first generate Bodhi Mind. Bodhi Mind has two aspects, aspirational and operational. We will explore aspirational Bodhi Mind first by studying its five components.

The first component of aspirational Bodhi Mind is the non-abandonment of living beings, which insures that the Bodhisattva Vow is not lost or degenerated. The Buddha has said that if we understand this one dharma, or teaching, we will understand all the dharmas. Let us say we have been repeatedly bothered and harmed by a certain person, in fact so often that we reach the point where we think that if there were ever a chance to help this person we would refuse to give help. If harm actually came to them and in some way we could stop it and we did not, then that is what is called abandoning a living being. We must strive never to do this.

The Buddha taught that the world could become a wonderful place if we could always feel love and concern towards any beings that caused us harm and that we should actually increase our feelings of compassion towards those beings. The nonabandoning of any other living being is the very basis of the Bodhi Mind. If we were to practice all the great deeds of the Bodhisattvas with extreme effort and diligence, the practice would not be proper if this first aspect were not kept. If at some point such a feeling should arise in us, it must immediately be acknowledged as an error so that the Bodhisattva Vow will not be degenerated and so that the cultivation of the Bodhi Mind is not hindered.

The second component of aspirational Bodhi Mind is the benefits that are associated with it. In one of the scriptures Maitreya speaks of the 130 different benefits of the Bodhi Mind. These may be abbreviated into four categories: first, the Bodhi Mind is like the seed of dharma; second, the practice of the Bodhi Mind alleviates the miseries of samsara and in this way it achieves our own purposes; third, the Bodhi Mind is the refuge for living beings and provides for the purposes of others rather than our own; and fourth, the Bodhi Mind is like a great general who defeats the enemy, the negative, afflicted emotions.

If we truly understand these benefits, we will actually have no difficulty in generating the Bodhi Mind and maintaining it. Since the Bodhi Mind has the benefit of achieving all positive things, it is compared to the wish-fulfilling gem which grants what one desires from the deepest part of one's heart. It is also compared to the Wonderful Vase. There is a tradition that the gods possess an extraordinary vase that grants the wishes and desires of anyone who wishes upon it. All living beings desire happiness and because the Bodhi Mind bestows happiness it is compared to the Wonderful Vase.

The third component of aspirational Bodhi Mind is the accumulation of merit and wisdom. *Merit* is accumulated through virtuous activities of the body, speech, and mind. Prostrations and circumambulating develop the virtues of the body, recitation of mantras and sutras accumulate the virtues of speech, and developing the power of samadhi through visualizing the deities produces the virtues of the mind. In generating aspirational Bodhi Mind, practicing the first five of the six paramitas (all the paramitas excluding Wisdom) are included in the Accumulation of Merit.

Wisdom is accumulated by the activity of dedicating merit to the ultimate perfection of all living beings. We do not hold on to accumulated merit for ourselves but give it over to each and every living being. When this is done, we make an effort to realize the emptiness of the three spheres which are: ourselves who are dedicating this merit; the merit which is being dedicated; and the object of the dedication, mainly living beings. Through meditation we realize these three spheres to be empty and devoid of any intrinsic reality. They are like an illusion, a dream. When the accumulation of merit and wisdom are perfected, we come to the point of realizing the true nature of all phenomena to be devoid of any natural, intrinsic existence. Being freed from this great delusion of the reality of substances, the great energy arises which powers the activities of the Bodhi Mind.

The fourth component of aspirational Bodhi Mind is the repeated practice of its various elements, the causal, the substantive, and the active. The causal element involves continually contemplating or meditating on compassion and loving kindness for all living beings. After taking the Bodhisattva Vow, we practice the creation or development of this great compassion and loving kindness for all beings three times when we get up in the morning and three times when we go to bed at night.

The substantive element is the repeated practice of generating Bodhi Mind with the motivation of attaining the state of perfect Buddhahood in order to best serve all living beings. There are many different prayers and ceremonies involved in the generation of this wish. Atisha taught the brief prayer which also can be said three times during the day and three times during the night. In Tibetan, that prayer is:

> Sanggye chö dang tsok kyi chok namla.
> Jangchub bardu dak ni kyab su chi.
> Dak gi jin sok gyi pei sönam kyi.
> Drola pen chir sanggye drub par shok.

The translation of this prayer in English is, "In the Buddha, Dharma, and Sangha I take refuge until I reach Enlightenment. By the merit of this practice of generosity and so forth, may I achieve Buddhahood for the benefit of all beings."

The active element involves continually dedicating our own body, our pleasures, and virtues to the benefit of others. We must always be mindful of our behavior, our sins, and our conflicting emotions.

The repeated practice of these three elements serves to increase the development of Bodhi Mind. As the Bodhi Mind increases from great to greater, selfishness and the ego become less and less. Finally when selfishness and the holding to ego has been reduced to the point of elimination, at that very moment, we achieve liberation.

The fifth and final component of aspirational Bodhi Mind is abandoning the four negative practices and cultivating the four positive practices. The four negative practices to be abandoned are: to abandon any deception of our lama, our teacher or any person we honor, such as our parents or those responsible for our training; to abandon rejecting the virtues of others; to abandon criticizing another being; and to abandon the deception of other beings, including attributing to others our bad actions or claiming others' good actions as our own. Because of the nature of these four negative practices, their repetition will inevitably cause the wearing away and finally the total destruction of the Bodhi Mind.

The corresponding four virtues which must be cultivated are: to cultivate not telling lies; to cultivate the practice of welcoming and even exhorting other people to practice virtue and especially to practice the Mahayana path; to cultivate respect for those beings who have generated Bodhi Mind as though they were the Buddha himself, announcing this quality to the Ten Directions; and to cultivate honesty and sincerity toward all beings and avoid deceiving other beings.

The aspirational Bodhi Mind is summed up in these five components and should be carefully studied and understood. If we go over them again and again in our minds and become aware of all the different subtle qualities involved in each of the components, we can easily generate the aspirational Bodhi Mind. We must always remember that the most important component is the first one, the non-abandonment of any living being. The development of the Bodhi Mind is the very heart and soul of the Mahayana path. It is the very essence of the path to Buddhahood which cannot be attained without it.

When we hear about the Vajrayana, the Vehicle of the Secret Mantra, we must not neglect the cultivation of the Bodhi Mind, because the Vajrayana can never be practiced until the Bodhi Mind has been cultivated and thoroughly developed. In the Vehicle of the Secret Mantra, there are many deities in the wrathful form which must be visualized and meditated upon and this can be very dangerous if we have not first perfected Bodhi Mind. Once we have developed Bodhi Mind, the practice of the Vajrayana comes naturally and we succeed in it. We become able to relieve not only our own sufferings but also those of other beings. Besides guiding ourselves to the place of liberation, we become the object of refuge for living beings and are able to free them from miseries as well as guide them to liberation.

It is vital to remember that these teachings are not given just to inform us, but are the point of departure for our active practice. If we do not carefully contemplate and investigate this teaching for ourselves, as well as put it into practice, then it is meaningless.

Questions

If we are angry with someone, are we abandoning them?

There are many different degrees of anger. If we feel anger towards another being, it does not necessarily mean that we are abandoning them. For instance if a child does some bad thing and the parent gets angry at the child, it is not abandoning the child. The abandoning we are speaking of is when, from the depth of our hearts, we wish to harm another being or wish to see some difficulty or trouble come to them.

Quite often we get angry with another being just because we are involved with them and wish to help them. We feel frustrated when they do something wrong, but this anger comes from our concern with helping them and is not what is called abandoning. Let us say we have a young child that plays hooky and hangs out smoking cigarettes and drinking beer. If we respond to his actions with very gentle words and say, "Oh, that's all right. You're a good boy. Do whatever you want," then within the child's lifetime he will certainly suffer greatly because of this pattern of behavior. On the other hand, if we make a show of great anger and force the child to clean up and go to school and behave properly, great benefit will come to the child because of that. Of course we also must be careful of going to the other extreme and showing great anger carelessly when it is not motivated through concern and loving kindness.

The only way you can tell if a person is in truth abandoning a living being is by looking at their heart and mind to see what they really desire. In one of the sutras the Buddha stated, "Only I and those who are like me, that is, those who have attained completely perfected Buddhahood, can accurately see into the minds of other beings." Based upon this we can see how wrong it is to blame or accuse other beings when we do not know what is truly in their hearts.

The great teacher Nagarjuna compared looking into the heart and mind of others with a certain type of fruit. This fruit is very deceptive. Sometimes the outside looks ripe but it is not ripe inside; other times the inside is ripe but the outside looks unripened. Then at times, the condition of the fruit is accurately reflected by the skin. Just as we cannot judge the true ripeness of this fruit by its skin, so we also are unable to judge the nature of another's motivations by appearances alone. We must have true insight into the situation.

How do we meditate on compassion?

The meditation consists of sitting down and thinking about all living beings. Consider their misery and generate within yourself compassion and a concern to both alleviate their misery and establish them in a state of perfect happiness. It is a mental practice. What you are aiming for is a sincere development of this feeling in your mind. With meditation and prayer it is the mental quality that is important. If you are sincerely thinking about obtaining perfect enlightenment for the sake of helping living beings, then this thought will automatically arise even when you are sleeping. This way it develops day and night and each day it is stronger than the day before.

Can you combine this meditation and Atisha's prayer?

You may combine them in the sense of doing them at the same time but you should recognize the separate aspects of what you are doing. In other words you are first developing the feeling of overwhelming compassion to alleviate the misery of living beings; second, wishing to establish them in a state of happiness; and third, reciting the prayer of Atisha.

Could you explain what the emptiness of the three spheres is?

This is the process of dedicating the merit which has been accumulated. It cannot remain as an accumulation because that would be doing something with a very dualistic mind. There would be myself who has accumulated the merit and other living beings who receive it, and because of that distinction it is very dualistic, that is, it assumes the reality of self and other. The emptiness of the three spheres means dedicating the merit and cultivating the awareness that these distinctions are not real but mere illusions. These illusions are caused by our own ignorance when we think that there is a self that is dedicating this merit, or that there is some intrinsic substance of merit, or that there is some intrinsic existent being to whom the merit is being dedicated. All three are empty and lack any intrinsic existence.

Where is merit accumulated? How do we know if we are accumulating it?

Accumulating virtue is effortless. Even the smallest virtue can be accumulated if we dedicate the merit. This is just like when we put money in the bank and it accumulates interest without us having to worry about it. It just naturally accumulates. The "merit bank" is empty space. This is the big bank, completely inexhaustible. As long as you are dedicating the merit, you don't have to be concerned with accumulating. Your mind, your body, and your view of the external world will tell you whether virtues are being accumulated. Everything will become more beautiful, peaceful, and gentle as the virtues make the nonvirtues powerless. If you cling to your virtues and do not dedicate them, they will be exhausted. Anytime your emotions come, you can say "good-bye" to your merit if you are holding to it. If you have a very fine crystal glass, you are always careful not to break it. However, if you hold on too tightly, a little bump can shatter the glass instantly. If you are virtuous and do not cling to the virtue, but do not dedicate it either, no merit is accumulated. The virtue will last only as long as the deed.

You mentioned we must have pure motivation in our practice. How can we maintain a pure motivation all the time?

First of all you must understand that what we are talking about is the high motivation of the Mahayana and that we are undertaking this practice, or whatever religious practice, for the sake of actually obtaining enlightenment ourselves in order to help all sentient beings. We generate this motivation very strongly, very purely, without any doubt whatsoever that we will attain Buddhahood and thus gain the power to alleviate the miseries of every last being. This is pure motivation.

There are three parts to any religious practice. There is the preparation, the reason for undertaking the religious practice; there is the actual practice; and there is the concluding practice. Whenever you do any work, be it religious or not, you set about it with some purpose in mind. This is your motivation and once you have it, you act upon it. When you meditate, you meditate; when you are saying a prayer, you just say the prayer; when you are doing some Bodhisattva activity, you just do it in a total unity of mind and purpose, because you are involved in an activity that was begun with pure motivation. The practice of the Buddhist religion, and in particular the Mahayana practice, always has these three parts: the Bodhisattva motivation, the actual practice, and the conclusion, which is the dedication of merit.

What do we do when we break our Boddhisattva Vow?

Confession of any degeneration of the Bodhisattva Vow is necessary again and again. Once you have taken the Bodhisattva Vow from your spiritual teacher, you must take it again every morning. There are specific prayers for confessing any faults you have in the degeneration of your vow, in particular the Confession before the Thirty-five Buddhas. This can be found in the pamphlet *Maintaining the Bodhisattva Vow and the Bodhicitta Precepts* (KDK Publications, 1984). In particular it is important to confess before your lama and also to the Bodhisattvas.

Chapter Two
Operational Bodhi Mind

The best way to understand the Bodhi Mind in its two aspects, the aspirational component and the actual practice or operational component, is through a metaphor. If we wish to take a trip to India, we will go through two phases in attaining our goal. The first phase is a mental one. We get the idea that we want to go to India and we think about the ways we could get there. This is analogous to aspirational Bodhi Mind.

The second phase is an active one. We set out upon the road to India. The journey, from the very first step we take until we actually arrive in India, is analogous to the operational aspect of Bodhi Mind. Both aspects must be present for the completion of any goal or task. We must first have the thought to accomplish the task and make the mental preparation of considering how to do it. Next we have the actual involvement in which we are working towards that goal and doing whatever is necessary to fulfill it. Both of these aspects are equally important and absolutely necessary.

Operational Bodhi Mind is divided into special ethics, special concentration, and special wisdom. In Tibetan, these are called La Pa Sum, the three special things, and they have a particular correspondence to the six paramitas or six perfections. Special ethics includes the first three of the paramitas: the perfection of generosity, the perfection of ethics and morals, and the perfection of patience. Special concentration is comprised of the fifth perfection, concentration. Special wisdom is comprised of the sixth perfection, wisdom. The fourth perfection, diligence, does not belong exclusively to any of the three special things but is necessary to all three; it is the catalyst which causes all three to work.

The six perfections, which form the actual practice of the Bodhi Mind, may be viewed in two ways. The first is the detailed and subtle explanation of each of the six perfections, which will be presented in the next six chapters. The second view is the presentation in brief, which is given in this chapter. The presentation in brief has six categories: divisions, levels, individual characteristics, etymology, structure, and the summation.

Divisions involves two constituents of the dharma practice, forms of higher rebirth such as humans and gods, and the ultimate goal of Buddhahood. The perfections of generosity, ethics and morals, and patience belong to the higher life forms. Generosity is the cause of wealth and enjoyment; ethics and morals are the cause of the physical body (and the qualities of that body are dependent upon our level of practice of ethics); and patience determines our surroundings and those among whom we take rebirth. These three are the seeds of life in the higher realms.

The perfections of diligence, meditative concentration, and wisdom belong to the goal of Buddhahood. Diligence is the cause of the acquisition and development of all good and higher qualities; meditative concentration is the cause of mastering and calming the mind; and wisdom is the cause of perfect insight or vipasyana. These three are the seeds of the final goal.

Levels defines the stages of our own mental development

along this path to enlightenment. The way in which the six paramitas function in our own mental continuum is in a graduated order. First there is the perfection of generosity which, when practiced, develops naturally into ethics and morals. This occurs as we begin to develop a charitable, generous, and liberal attitude by bestowing things upon the needy. We automatically develop a sense of nonattachment, thereby overcoming our greed and developing a sense of kindness and compassion for others. The obstacles to ethical and moral practice are such things as greed, clinging to possessions, and lack of compassion, so by developing a generous attitude we overcome the obstacles to an ethical and moral practice.

When we practice ethics and morals, patience naturally follows. Patience in turn produces great diligence, and diligence leads to meditative concentration. This leads to the development of wisdom whereby one gains analytical and penetrating insight into the actual nature of reality.

Another way of viewing these levels would be from lowest to highest, with generosity being first and lowest and wisdom being last and highest. We cannot begin the practice by studying wisdom; that would be impossible. We start at the bottom by practicing generosity and charity, and gradually work our way up to the practice of wisdom. Another description of these levels is that they are graduated from gross to subtle. In the beginning we don't understand the subtle features of our practice, but we can see and practice the gross ones. As we improve and extend our practice, it naturally becomes more and more subtle.

There are four *individual characteristics* of the Six Paramitas. First, these perfections serve to eliminate all opposition to our progress toward enlightenment. Second, they produce in our minds the insight which is not confused by conceptualization. Third, they fulfill our wish for the temporary and ultimate happiness of all living beings.

Fourth, they fulfill others' wishes for happiness.

Etymology describes the meaning of the names of the Six Perfections. The etymology of the words chinpa in Tibetan and dana in Sanskrit is giving, generosity or charity. This perfection of generosity is concerned with the clearing away of the poverty of living beings.

˙The etymology of the words tsultrim (Tib.) and sila (Skt.) is religious conduct or moral law. This perfection of ethics and morals clears away or cools the burning heat of the afflicted passions.

The etymology of the words söpa (Tib.) and ksanti (Skt.) is to suffer, bear or endure. This perfection of patience endures the wrath of others.

The etymology of the words tsontru (Tib.) and virya (Skt.) is industry or assiduity. This perfection of diligence eliminates the obstacles to both the temporal and final goals of ourselves and others.

The etymology of samten (Tib.) and dhyana (Skt.) is the state of complete attention or contemplation. This perfection of meditative concentration causes the mind to be self-possessed, avoiding distractions and illusory phenomena.

The etymology of the words sherab (Tib.) and prajna (Skt.) is absolute wisdom or understanding. This perfection of wisdom enables us to see reality as it actually is.

The Six Paramitas are called "perfections" because they are the practices which enable us to cross the ocean of samsara, the ocean of misery. At the other shore of the ocean is the perfect state of Buddhahood.

The *structure* of the perfections is that each is connected to all the others, forming thirty-six subdivisions. For example, there is the generosity of generosity, the generosity of ethics, the generosity of patience, the generosity of diligence, the generosity of meditative concentration, and the generosity of wisdom. In the second perfection there is the ethics of generosity, the ethics of ethics, the ethics of patience, the ethics of diligence, the ethics of meditative concentration, and the ethics of wisdom. When this structure is repeated with each of the Six Perfections, it forms the thirty-six subdivisions.

An example of the generosity of generosity is when we give something to someone. We make the prayer that, just as this one being has been benefited, so may all beings be benefited, not only in this small way but also in the ultimate way by being in the possession of perfect Buddhahood.

An example of the generosity of ethics would be that when we give a gift we do so in a moral way. Instead of giving with the aim of getting something back in the future, we give only with the pure feeling of helping this being.

The generosity of patience means that when we give some gift we do so without minding any difficulties which might arise from this act of charity or generosity. We are willing to endure any hardships to be able to give this gift.

The generosity of diligence means that we not only give the gift, but do so without any laziness, without postponing it, and without letting any obstacle prevent our generosity.

The generosity of meditative concentration is to perform our act of giving with an undistracted mind. We one-pointedly concentrate upon benefiting living beings by our gift.

The generosity of wisdom means we perform the act of giving with a thorough awareness of the emptiness of the giver, the gift, and the receiver.

The final category of the presentation in brief of the Six Paramitas is the *summation.* The Six Perfections are incorporated into the Two Accumulations, merit and wisdom. Generosity and ethics are included in the accumulation of merit and the perfection of wisdom is included in the accumulation of wisdom. The remaining three perfections, patience, diligence, and meditative concentration, are included in both accumulations.

Questions

Where does the energy or the ability to practice the paramitas come from?

The ability to practice these perfections is based upon your own karma. If you totally lack the karma from former activities, from former existences, then you do not embark upon the practice of these perfections. For example, if you were building a house, it would not be possible to finish it in one day. But that's all right because you can take up where you left off at the beginning of the next day. So likewise with the practice of the paramitas, if you in a former lifetime have laid the foundation and done a certain amount of work, then naturally in this life you will take up where you left off. Without the preliminary basis of activities leading up to this practice, it would be very rare to take it up in this lifetime.

The fact that you are interested in the practice of the paramitas and that you have come to investigate them is dependent upon the karma of your own former lifetimes. Since you do have that basis of former karma and can now take up these practices, you must take them up diligently, for the nature of this karma or of any karma is that soon it will become exhausted and you will lose the opportunity.

Are there any texts on the paramitas that we can read?

There are several basic texts on the paramitas. One is *Dam Chö Yid Shin Norbu Tarpa Rinpoche Gyen*. This text is easily available in English under the title *Jewel Ornament of Liberation* by Gampopa (translated by Herbert V. Guenther,

Shambala, 1971). Another text is the *Bodhicharyavatara* by Shantideva. This Mahayana text is accepted by all schools and is recommended by His Holiness the Dalai Lama as the best one on the subject. It is presently available in English under the title *A Guide to the Bodhisattva's Way of Life* by Shantideva (translated by Stephen Batchelor, Library of Tibetan Works and Archives, Dharamsala, 1979) and as *Entering the Path to Enlightenment* (translated by Marion Mates, Allen & Unwin, London, 1970). In addition, a commentary by Geshe Kelsang Gyatso, *Meaningful to Behold,* is available through Wisdom Publications.

This presentation of the Six Paramitas is drawn from many sources not presently available in English. It is offered for the student who cannot read the traditional texts and contains enough information to begin the practice of the paramitas.

The vase represents generosity.

Chapter Three
Generosity

With the perfection of generosity, we begin the extensive and detailed explanation of the paramitas. This broad presentation is composed of seven parts. First we will look at the detriments of not practicing and the benefits of practicing generosity; second, the nature of generosity; third, the classifications of generosity; fourth, the defining characteristics of generosity; fifth, the increase of generosity; sixth, the purification of generosity; and seventh, the results of the practice of generosity.

The *detriments of not practicing and the benefits of practicing generosity* are concerned with both temporary and ultimate results. The temporary and immediate detriment of a lack of generosity is that if we are without virtue, we are miserable and suffer from deprivation in this very lifetime. We impoverish ourselves through not giving and feel unhappy and deprived. In this state, we are in no position to help others and when we do not accomplish the purposes of others, we do not make spiritual progress and cannot approach the path leading to perfect Buddhahood. So the immediate result of the lack or detriment of not giving is the obstruction of our spiritual progress.

The ultimate effect of the lack of generosity in the next

lifetime is that we will take rebirth in the hungry ghost realm of beings who are tormented by hunger, thirst, and other deprivations. Even if we are able to attain human rebirth, it will be in a very miserable condition.

The temporary benefits of the practice of giving are that we will enjoy excellent possessions and conditions in this life. The great teacher Nagarjuna once wrote a letter to a friend discussing the benefits of generosity. This letter has since been called the *Superlative,* or the *Friendly Letter.* He said that there is no antidote to unwholesome activities and the defilements of sin that is more effective than the practice of generosity. In the Gurma scripture it is taught that every living being throughout the universe desires the same thing, that is, happiness. Happiness arises from practicing charity toward others. We become free of deprivation and in this blessed condition we attract the very best surroundings, the best situation of friends, relatives and people around us, and further we establish the causes of the attainment of perfect Buddhahood. Because generosity fulfills the actual wishes of all living beings, the Buddha Shakyamuni taught generosity as the very first practice of the paramitas.

In answer to the questions of a certain householder, the Buddha also taught that whatever we give to others is truly ours and whatever we keep for ourselves we will lose. When we give things away, they are never exhausted, because the good effect persists; when we hoard them, they will quickly disappear.

The ultimate benefits of giving are that through this practice we close the door to our own rebirth in the hungry ghost realms. By being generous, we also cut the causes of our own misery and deprivation and that of other living beings.

Understanding the **nature of generosity** is quite simple. It is defined as whatever we hold as our own possession, whatever we identify as belonging to us. This is the nature of what we must give.

There are three *classifications of generosity:* the giving of material gifts, the giving of fearlessness, and the giving of dharma. Material gifts are given to make firm or benefit the physical body, fearlessness is given to make the lifespan more secure, and dharma is given to make the mind secure. The first two of these, material gifts and fearlessness, are given to benefit living beings in this very life; dharma is given to benefit beings in future lives by the attainment of perfect Buddhahood. Because of their ultimate benefit, the gifts of dharma are considered to be the most precious of gifts.

These three classifications of gifts are examined more closely in the discussion of *defining characteristics.* Material gifts fall into two subdivisions, pure gifts and impure gifts. There are four kinds of impure gifts: gifts given with impure thought; gifts which are impure in substance; gifts given to an impure recipient; and gifts given in an impure way.

There are two kinds of gifts given with impure thoughts, those that are perverted and those that are base or mean. We give with perverted thought if we give to harm someone, to benefit ourselves, to gain a good reputation for ourselves, or if we give with a jealous motivation. We give with base or mean thought when we give to gain wealth or higher rebirth for ourselves.

The kinds of gifts which are impure in substance include any objects which could cause harm to any living being, or any instruction which could lead to harm. For example, a gun is a gift that might harm, and instructing someone in the use of a gun would also be impure. Another gift which is improper because of its substance is the gift of our relatives, or someone over whom we have power, without their consent.

The next type of impure gift is one which is improper because of the recipient. This would include giving our body or parts of our body to another being who asks to use them for some perverted purpose. If we were to fulfill this wish of some demonic, possessed, or insane being, we would not help the recipient but would contribute to their eventual harm. We would also deprive ourselves of the precious human body which is the vehicle to enlightenment for the sake of all living beings. Another example of an improper recipient is a gluttonous or drunken person asking for food or drink. We do not give to them, as this would contribute to their harm.

The last kind of impure gift is that which is given in an improper way. To give a gift out of anger or while despising the recipient for being miserable or poor, or to give with harsh language, is improper. When our giving is primarily motivated by any of the five poisons of ignorance, anger, desire, jealousy, or pride, we are giving the gift improperly.

There are three types of pure gifts. Some gifts are pure because of substance, some because of their recipient, and some because of the method of giving. Those gifts pure in substance are further divided into inner and outer gifts. Inner gifts are those which are closest to us all, our own flesh and blood. Bodhisattvas can give of their flesh and blood when it is needed and thus can give the inner gifts. There is a story of one of Nagarjuna's disciples, Arya Deva, who was challenged to a religious debate by a leading Hindu scholar of his day. Traveling to the debate, Arya Deva met a blind man. Now this blind man had been stationed on the road by the Hindu scholar who knew that Arya Deva's compassion for this man would cause him to give up his own eyes, making him unable to complete his journey to the debate. Arya Deva, who had realized his ultimate sameness with others, easily removed his eyes and placed them in the blind man's empty sockets. His accomplishment was so great that he was able to continue his journey and win the debate.

It is important for us to understand that, although we may have set out on the Bodhisattva Path, until we obtain a certain stage of skill and wisdom, such inner gifts as Arya Deva's are beyond our capability. Specifically, until we obtain the realization of the exchange of self and other, we are unable to give this type of gift.

Although we cannot give parts of our bodies, such as arms, legs, eyes, or organs, we can give the inner gift of the use of the whole body. For example, when someone asks us to get a glass of water or do some other task, we "give" our body by using it as the instrument to accomplish the request. We should, however, keep our precious human body alive until we know for certain that sacrificing it will attain more benefit for beings than living out our lives on the Bodhisattva Path. We must be very careful not to think ourselves invulnerable when we consider endangering our precious human body. Each one of us has read stories of attempted rescues of drowning people in which the rescuers become drowning victims themselves. This is not giving a gift but throwing away a precious life.

Pure substantial gifts of the outer variety include whatever we possess or control such as money, clothes, or food.

The second type of pure gift, that which is pure because of the recipient, has four divisions: excellence, kindness, deprivation, and harm. The division of excellence is determined by the quality of being able to lead oneself and other beings out of the realms of samsara. These excellent recipients of giving include lamas and the Three Jewels, Buddha, Dharma, and Sangha. Giving to this first division is very important.

The division of kindness includes those beings who have helped us, such as our parents. They have shown us great kindness and giving to them is a way to return their kindness.

The division of deprivation encompasses all living beings because all are deprived of happiness as they wander through the realms of samsara undergoing the manifold miseries that are involved in such wandering. All living beings are proper recipients of our gifts as they are eternally deprived of happiness; we must seek to relieve their misery in any way we can.

The division of harm entails giving to those who would harm us. They are proper recipients of our gifts if we can truly benefit them and not harm ourselves. For example, if we have food and someone wants it, we should give it to them if we have enough and will not be harmed by the gift. If, however, we have taken a vow to do meditation all day and this is our only meal, it is better to keep the food, because our meditation will benefit all beings.

When we look at the third type of gift, those which are pure because of the method by which they are given, we look at excellence in motivation and excellence in operation. Excellence in motivation is being moved by compassion for another's need and seeking to relieve their misery by our generosity. We do this not just to relieve this one being's misery, but that of all beings, and we seek to bring about the happiness not only of this one being, but that of all beings. Finally we must think that this happiness should not be temporary but the ultimate happiness that comes with the attainment of perfect and fearless enlightenment. If this entire train of thought is present, we have what is called the excellence in motivation.

Excellence in operation is the proper attitude in the act of giving the gift. In order for our attitude to be excellent we must first rejoice in the three times. This means rejoicing before the gift is given (at the time of contemplating giving), rejoicing at the time of giving the gift by having a pure mind completely unaffected by any of the klesas, and, after giving the gift, having no trace of regret at having parted with the gift.

The second requirement of excellence in operation is respect. This means having the respectful attitude of the body, speech, and mind. The mind is thinking, "May this bring true happiness," the speech is gentle and kind, and the body is acting in a respectful and gentle manner.

The third requirement is that we must give with our own hand instead of employing someone else to give the gift and we must also give at the right time, that is, whenever we have something to give.

To complete excellence in operation, we must do no harm with our gifts, that is, take from one person and give to another, or deprive one person in order to give to another. Also we must not give gifts involving other beings, such as giving relatives or children away without their consent. If all these attitudes are observed in the action of giving, then we have excellence in operation.

A final note on the topic of material gifts comes from the Abidharma of Maitreya. We are encouraged to practice giving by doing it repeatedly, to give impartially to all beings, and to give wisely and appropriately for the greatest good.

The classification of the generosity of fearlessness means that we must give refuge and protection to beings and eliminate their fears. In this classification, the very greatest gift is returning life to a being. For example, we might go to a market and find some type of animal or fish that is alive, but is about to be taken out and killed for someone's meal. We can purchase this being and return it to its natural habitat, thus returning its liberty and life.

Another way to give the gift of fearlessness would be to offer protection to a being that fears some great punishment. If we see a child being abused, we would be giving the gift of fearlessness if we called the proper authorities and did what we could to protect the child. However, it is important at our level of practice to be very skillful in the ways that we offer this protection. We should not endanger our precious human opportunity, our lineage, and our faith by our efforts. For example, if someone has been apprehended for some crime and is facing a great punishment, we must do what we can to allay their fears or lessen their suffering. This does not mean that we can break the law; that would only get us, our lineage, and Buddhism in trouble.

In general then, whenever we can protect some being from what they fear, whether that is water, fire, wild animals, or great punishment, we are giving the gift of fearlessness.

The final classification of generosity is the gift of dharma. The defining characteristics of this gift involve four subdivisions: object, motivation, substance, and method.

The object is the proper recipient to whom the gift of dharma is given. This is a being who has faith and devotion in the dharma and in those who teach the dharma. If we know someone who is simply curious, we can share our own experience of the teacher, lineage, and dharma. We can then connect them with our teacher for further information. Sharing our experiences and connecting them with our teacher is giving the gift of dharma at our own level.

Motivation is divided into two categories, nonvirtuous and virtuous. The nonvirtuous involves giving the gifts of dharma with the idea of gaining some respect, honor, or fame. Virtuous motivation is giving the gift of dharma with compassion, with the desire to relieve the recipient of misery, and in particular, with the intention to clear away the great miseries which arise from the five afflicted emotions, the klesas.

The substance of dharma gifts is the unconfused, inexhaustible and unerring dharma of the Buddha. It is the teaching of the three practices of study, contemplation, and meditation, and the gifts of merit and wisdom. Merit is the development of great compassion which encompasses all living beings and wisdom is the realization of the ultimate truth of shunyata (Tib: tong pa nyi). The method of giving the gifts of dharma is explained in the sutras. This gift is not to be casually or lightly given but is only given after careful examination of the prospective recipient. It must be ascertained that the recipient is requesting the dharma from a deep desire to learn the precious teachings and with a sense of faith and respect towards them. If they approach merely out of curiosity or for some less than wholesome reason, then the dharma will not help them because they are not listening with a pure motivation. Without pure motivation, it is not possible to truly understand the dharma. This belittling of the dharma can become a cause of rebirth in the lower realms.

If, after examination, we see that someone is an appropriate recipient for the dharma, we do not have to wait for a formal request for the teachings. It is our responsibility to give the teachings the moment it is ascertained that some being will benefit by them.

In the Sutra of the White Lotus, it is stated that the method of bestowing the gift of dharma involves arranging the proper setting for the teachings to be given. Cleaning the room, setting up the seat for the teacher properly, and arranging the room with paintings and statues of the Buddhas and the Bodhisattvas will make the teaching space very open to the blessings. Furthermore, the teacher of the dharma must have what is called proper behavior, that is, the teacher's manner and physical demeanor must be proper and conducive to the bestowing of the sacred teachings.

Next we will look at the *increase of generosity* which has three sections: insight, wisdom, and dedication. Insight involves understanding the lack of intrinsic reality of the three spheres, the giver, the recipient, and the gift. When the practitioner of generosity completely realizes the emptiness of these three spheres, then the gift becomes more than an ordinary one. In this way, giving is said to increase through insight.

The second section of the increase of generosity is called wisdom, and this is further divided into three subsections: motivation, nonattachment, and nonexpectation. Before the gift is given, our motivation must be that this gift will lead to the attainment of perfect enlightenment for the recipient and for all living beings. At the moment of giving, this gift is given with an attitude free of any trace of attachment or clinging to the substance of the gift. After the gift has been given, we must have an attitude free of any expectation of reward for having given the gift. When these three factors of wisdom are present, the gift becomes transcendent.

The third section of the increase of generosity is dedication. Dedication involves consecrating the gift and the virtue of giving it, not merely to the one being who has received it, but to all beings. Since beings are as limitless as space, and because we dedicate the gift to all beings, then the gift itself becomes limitless.

This method of consecrating the gift also means that the virtue of the gift is never exhausted until one has attained perfect Buddhahood. If a single drop of water is added to the ocean, that drop could not be lost unless the whole ocean dried up. So when we dedicate the merit of giving a gift to the supreme enlightenment, we cannot be said to have used up that merit or lost that merit until we have attained the perfect Buddhahood.

In the increase of generosity, then, we seek three actions. If we can see the gift as empty, we increase the generosity. If we can achieve nonattachment, the generosity becomes even greater. If we can dedicate the gift, the generosity becomes limitless. From this perspective, giving is done to realize emptiness and wisdom, not just to give. To simply "do good" without dedicating the merit means the virtue will be exhausted immediately. It may just go toward alleviating our bad karma. But if we dedicate the merit, we increase the virtue of doing good until it is inexhaustible.

In the *purification of generosity,* we strive to make giving a pure practice. The two agents which make the gift pure are shunyata (Tib: tong pa nyi) and compassion (Tib: nying je). Through the realization of shunyata, the gift does not become a part of or lead to samsara or samsaric activity. Through compassion the gift does not lead to or become a part of Hinayana practice.

The first of these agents, that of shunyata, was said by the Buddha to be composed of four seals which are stamped on the different items involved in giving. Those four items are material things, our own bodies, our own minds, and the dharma itself. Stamping material objects with the seal of shunyata means that we realize, first, that all material existence in the universe is illusory, without any inherent reality. Similarly we realize that our own bodies and our own minds are also without substantial existence. These realizations will stamp material things, our bodies and our minds with the seal of shunyata. When the dharma is seen to be without intrinsic reality and merely an expedient path that one travels to arrive at the state of perfect Buddhahood, and when Buddhahood itself is also seen to be without substantial existence, then the stamp of shunyata is placed upon all aspects of the dharma. When these four seals are applied to material objects, body, mind, and dharma, then all faults which lead to continued samsaric existence, or lead the gift to become a samsaric activity are removed. When applying these four seals, we first begin with an intellectual understanding of shunyata. When we have finally accomplished the realization, then the door to samsaric activity is actually sealed.

The second agent of the purification of generosity is compassion. When the gift that we give is motivated by a feeling of wishing to relieve another being of misery, and is extended to encompass all living beings wandering helplessly throughout samsara, then the gift does not become a Hinayana activity nor lead to the Hinayana path.

In conclusion, when shunyata and compassion are applied to giving, they are said to be cleaning agents and in this way they purify generosity.

The final category of generosity is *the results of the practice of giving.* There are two types of results, the ultimate and the temporary. The ultimate result of the practice of the paramita of generosity is the accomplishment of the state of perfect Buddhahood.

The temporary results of giving are seen in this lifetime and nearby lifetimes. Without even desiring it, we will be endowed with enjoyments and wealth. Many beings will gather around us and, because of this, we will be able to engage in virtuous activities and encourage others to do so. Thus we can accomplish the purposes of others.

Each specific kind of gift also has its own result. In the category of material gifts, if we give food, we will have good physical health; if we give clothing, we will have an attractive body; if we give candles or lights, we will have good eyesight and wisdom; if we give vehicles, we will have a pleasant dwelling.

When we give the gifts of fearlessness, we will be freed from obstacles in the future such as malicious beings who seek to harm us or bar our progress. We will be free from them and from other obstacles and be able to quickly advance towards enlightenment. The result of giving the gifts of dharma is that more profound teachings of the dharma will be available to us and, in the future, we will obtain a rebirth in which we are very close to the Buddha. We will be able to obtain his teachings directly and advance very rapidly on the path.

This concludes the teaching on the paramita of giving and we should go out and start giving gifts right away.

Questions

If I am having difficulty giving a gift because of thinking too much about it, what should I do?

It is good to consider gifts and to think about them. The teachings on generosity are given as a guide to enable you to understand when and how and to whom it is proper to give a gift. If you study and think about these teachings, they will clear up any doubts you have, for that is their purpose. This teaching will help you spontaneously know what to do, so you will have much less of this problem.

I have a problem that sometimes comes up. Sometimes people want my pechas (texts) and mala (rosary). Sometimes I give my pechas but I am reluctant to give my mala. Is it all right to keep it?

The Buddha gave many teachings on the subject of which things are fitting to give and which are not. For instance, for monks and nuns he taught that it is not fitting to give their begging bowl or their religious robe. These are not proper objects of giving. For the householder, ordinary people who are not monks or nuns, there are also restrictions. In general, it is not fitting to give anything which is a requirement for accomplishing virtue or helping others. So you have to look very carefully at each situation.

If you have a pecha which you read every day or if you have a mala that you say mantras on all the time and someone comes and thinks they are sort of pretty and would just like to have them but is not going to make any real use of them, then perhaps that's not a fitting person to give them to. The virtue you would accomplish through their use and the benefit to others would be greater if you held on to them. As the Buddha taught, the key issue is, "What is going to be most beneficial?"

Is it possible to give a gift of truth to a friend in the form of criticism if I see something in my friend that needs improvement, something in his own personality?

Giving criticism to someone who needs it, if it comes from both a sincere attitude of helping and also a true understanding, can be a good thing. However the most important thing is the attitude with which it is given. If it comes deeply from an attitude of wishing to help, wishing to benefit another being, then it is good; it is based upon the enlightened attitude of Bodhi Mind. As far as being included in the practice of generosity, we can't say that it is, unless it involves the giving of actual dharma teaching.

If you give a criticism to someone and say, "What you are doing is very wrong, so don't do it. Do something else," and if by following your advice this person becomes happy and has some benefit, still you have to look at what type of benefit, what type of happiness. If it is very elusive, delusive, worldly, temporary happiness, then it does not come under the heading of dharma and is not truly benefiting them. It is very important to look first at your motivation and your desire to help and then at your understanding of what's actually helpful to him.

If somebody comes up to me in the street and begs, I may or may not hand them some money. If I don't, is that an obstruction to the development of generosity?

When you see people like that and feel that it is not really correct to give to them or that you just don't feel like giving to them, as long as you don't do anything negative, just refrain from giving, you are not producing any merit but no sin, so that's o.k. It is important to understand that the root of generosity is compassion for another being, the wish for them to be happy. It might be that you feel that giving to them at this time and in this way is not the proper way to accomplish this end, but still it is important to feel the compassion. If you are able to give and circumstances seem to indicate that by giving you would relieve someone's misery, then you should be diligent in giving or at least have this feeling of compassion.

So then it probably would be beneficial to give something to them and overcome this feeling of not wanting to give?

It's always taught that generosity and charity are very important. It's very, very good and especially to give with a pure mind is very good. So whenever you can practice charity you should do so. Even if you only have a few cents, if you give it with the attitude that the benefit is very great, it is as if you were giving thousands of dollars. The chief thing is the attitude.

If I am very wealthy and think, "I'll give this person a thousand dollars, and then people will respect me and think I'm really something," and I give the money without the motivation to benefit all beings, the gift is not very great because the proper attitude is missing. Your gift of a few cents with the proper attitude is much greater. It is a cause of your own development toward the attainment of Buddhahood and thus is vastly more beneficial. Also, if you are unable to give to others because you have no money, but see someone else give a gift, and you have a feeling of rejoicing at seeing this act of charity, then the result is that you gain the merit of the gift. Whether the person giving the gift gave with a pure attitude or selfish impure attitude doesn't matter. You gain merit from your attitude.

Sometimes someone comes up to you and asks for money and you just give it to them. Do you have to go through that whole thing to make it count?

You mean someone just comes up to you and asks for some money and you have your life savings in your pocket and do you just reach in and give them $10,000?

I give them whatever I have to give.

If you have that attitude, and without thinking you just

take it out and give it to them, it may or may not be a good thing. Suppose you are not alone in the world, but instead have a family that is dependent on you and you give all your money away. Suppose this person doesn't really need it. Perhaps he's just out there to get some change for the bus or something. You are not really benefiting him and are doing harm to your family. It is important in any activity, especially when you are trying to practice the perfections, to have an attitude of caution and circumspection in whatever you do. You don't just reach in and give whatever you have if that keeps you from getting on the bus or getting to work. Take an instant to consider how much to give the person. It's also important when you take that second to consider what will really help this person and have this foremost in your mind.

To clarify the answer to your question, it is sometimes difficult for us, especially as beginners in these practices, to really think about the meaning and the motivation of our giving. If someone asks for some money, you don't just stop and wait awhile until you can generate this perfect attitude. The thing is that if you do give it to them, then later on as part of any practice you can dedicate the merit. You can generate this attitude and think, "May this virtue benefit all living beings; may this virtue help others to attain Buddhahood." However, it is very good if this attitude can be cultivated before you do the actual giving so that the actual process of giving comes from the deep wish to benefit this being and all other beings. We have to be practical in our way of giving. We have to do it in an effective way. It is not very effective if, when someone asks you for a gift, you think, 'Oh, I'll have to generate this Bodhisattva attitude of giving,'' and so you stop and sit down cross-legged and think for awhile. The person will probably think you are crazy and go away and the virtue will never be accomplished.

The lotus represents ethics and morality.

Chapter Four
Ethics and Morals

Continuing the extensive and detailed explanation of the paramitas, we come to the perfection of ethics and morals. As in the first paramita, this is divided into seven parts: the detriments of not practicing and the benefits of practicing ethics and morals; the nature of ethics and morals; classifications; defining characteristics; increase; purification; and results.

As a result of *not practicing ethics and morals,* we will not gain a higher rebirth in the next life as humans or gods, and we will not attain the state of leisure and opportunity in the next lifetime whereby we can practice the dharma. In this regard, it is written in the *Madhyamakavatara* (Tib: *Uma Chugpa*) that the person who has broken the leg of ethics and morals will not travel to their destination. In the practice of the dharma, ethics and morals are like our legs and feet. Just as a person who has broken a leg cannot walk down the path, so the person without ethics and morals cannot practice the dharma and thus falls into evil existences in future lifetimes. Furthermore, even though they practice generosity, they will fall into evil existences without the basis of ethics and morals. This would mean being endowed with property and enjoyments as a

101

result of their generosity but still experiencing lower rebirth in the animal, hungry ghost, or hell realms.

Another detriment of not practicing ethics and morals is that in the future we will not have the ability to meet with or come in contact with the teachings of the Buddha. In a certain sutra, *Silasamyuktasutra* (Tib: *Tsultrim then pay do*) which is the Sutra Regarding the Possession of Ethics and Morals, it is taught that just as a blind person cannot see forms, so a person without ethics and morals cannot see the dharma. The great detriment of not possessing and practicing ethics and morals is, in essence, that we will not be able to see the dharma and thus will not be able to tread the path to liberation or attain the final state of Buddhahood.

The **benefits of practicing ethics and morals** are that in the future we can obtain the precious human existence and be endowed with the leisure and opportunity to make spiritual progress and eventually attain the state of perfect Buddhahood. Ethics and morals are compared with the earth itself, for just as the earth is the support of all things that are mobile and immobile, so ethics and morals are the support for spiritual practice.

In the *Friendly Letter*, Nagarjuna taught that just as earth is the basis out of which all sustenance comes, so ethics and morals are the ground or basis out of which all virtues and spiritual attainments come. The person who is endowed with ethics and morals is the fertile field in which the seed of the dharma grows and flourishes. One virtue will lead to another and the accumulated merit will never be exhausted.

In the *Moon-illuminated Sutra* it is taught that the afflicted mental states of ignorance, desire, and hatred stir up the mind. Through practicing ethics and morals, we get rid of these afflictions and our minds naturally become quiet and tranquil, allowing the many levels of samadhi to be attained. Vipasyana, the pure insight into reality, naturally follows, and from this comes the attainment of omniscience and perfect Buddhahood. The foundation of all of this is the proper practice of ethics and morals.

Further benefits of practicing ethics and morals are described in the sutra *Pitaputrasamagamana* (Tib: *Yabsre jelwai do*), which says that through the practice of ethics and morals, the wishes of the mind are naturally obtained. In the temporary or immediate perspective, we attain happiness and pleasant conditions in this lifetime; in the future, we attain the greatest of our wishes, perfect Buddhahood. The sutra further states that the proper practice of ethics and morals will make the final perfection of Buddhahood something that is not far off, but easily and quickly approachable.

The *nature of ethics and morals* describes the right conduct of this perfection and has two sections, taking up and guarding. Taking up ethics and morals has two concerns. First, we must receive our instruction from someone who possesses a high sense of ethics and morals. It is our responsibility as students to watch and ask questions in order to find the possessors of ethics and morals. Second, our practice must arise from a high sense of resolve to benefit others rather than from the hope of fame or gain or high rebirth in the next lifetime.

Guarding ethics and morals also has two concerns. First, when we take up the practice of ethics and morals, it is important not to let the practice degenerate. If we make a mistake or transgress the moral code, it is important to confess it to our teacher and resolve not to do it again. Second, when we take up the practice of ethics and morals, we keep it constant by reminding ourselves of the importance of the practice, the benefits of practicing, and harm of not practicing.

The *classifications of ethics and morals* are threefold: constraint, cultivation of virtuous activities, and benefiting living beings. Observing the morality of constraint quiets the mind, causing it to abide within itself. Observing the morality of cultivating virtuous activities ripens the seed of the dharma within our own mental continuum. Without the practice of dharma and even after we begin to practice it, our minds are usually overcome with afflicted emotions. The seed of the dharma, even if present, does not flourish without the cultivation of virtuous activities. As the seed of dharma thrives, the afflicted emotional states subside and eventually disappear. In this way our minds approach the state of purity and perfection. Observing the morality of benefiting beings causes this same seed of the dharma to ripen within others in the same way that cultivating virtue causes it to ripen within us.

These three classifications are examined more closely in *defining characteristics.* Constraint is divided into two subdivisions, common and unique. Common ethics and morals of constraint are those held in common by all vehicles of Buddhism. In the *Bodhisattvabhumi* (Tib: *Chyangsa*) it is stated that the common ethics and morals are outlined in the *Pratimoksha.* This has six divisions, one for each variety of religious practitioner, from fully-ordained monk to lay practitioner.

The unique ethics and morals of constraint are those unique to the Mahayana. These practitioners would follow the Buddha's teachings which advised not to practice ethics and morals for the sake of obtaining the state of men or gods in the next lifetime; not to practice them for the sake of attaining respect, wealth, ease, or happiness in this or future lifetimes; and not to practice them for the purpose of reassuring oneself or protecting oneself from fear of evil existence or trouble in the next lifetime. The practice of ethics and morals should be taken up out of concern for all living beings and for the sake of attaining Buddhahood. When the constraints of ethics and morals are taken with this attitude, one is practicing the unique moral strength of the Mahayana.

The specific rules are very extensive and were enumerated by Shantideva, following the teachings of the *Akasagarbha Sutra* (Tib: *Namkhai nying poi do)*. In this sutra, there are 18 major transgressions and 253 general ones to be avoided. Beyond this are many hundreds of regulations for the fully-ordained monk. These regulations are rarely taught because they require a teacher who is specifically pure in all aspects of these moral and ethical constraints, and listeners who are specifically devoted to understanding and practicing these manifold rules.

Observing the morality which cultivates virtuous activities means taking the Bodhisattva Vow and practicing bodhisattva deeds while honoring all the appropriate ethical and moral obligations. In addition, there are other obligations incumbent upon those who observe the morality of cultivating virtuous activities. In the *Bodhisattvabhumi* of Asanga, the subject is treated very extensively. First, Asanga taught the three dharma activities, hearing, contemplation, and practice. It is the obligation of all practitioners to expose themselves to manifold teachings. This is done through hearing and studying the teachings, contemplating them, resolving any doubts about them, and putting them into practice. Next Asanga taught that we are obligated to show honor, respect, and give service to the spiritual teacher who is the embodiment of the Buddha. We are also obligated to serve and provide for those beings who are sick or in need of some direct assistance. We must also help any beings in whatever way is appropriate, especially by being generous without any thought of personal benefit. We must always notice the good qualities of others and express them publicly, while being careful to notice and make known our own faults and shortcomings. Next, when noticing the good deeds and virtues of others, we should welcome and rejoice in them without any sense of jealousy. It is important also to make offerings to the Buddha, Dharma, and Sangha with diligence and enthusiasm and to dedicate whatever virtue we do to benefit all living beings.

The practitioners of this bodhisattva morality must constantly have a sense of awareness in regard to all of their activities, guarding the doors of the senses and the doors of body, speech, and mind. In regard to this, the practitioner is also obligated when approaching a spiritual teacher to cut off any sense of hesitation or doubt about the qualities or abilities or activities of the spiritual teacher. We must treat the teacher with a full and wholehearted sense of respect and always guard against the arising of these doubts and hesitations. Finally, we must not become remiss at any point, and must practice these obligations with devotion and diligence.

In order to effectively practice the ethics and morals which benefit others, we must purify all the activities of our body, speech, and mind. When we abandon the defiled conditions and generate the pure activities of body, speech, and mind, this benefits us by purifying our practice and benefits others by generating faith and devotion in the dharma.

On a bodily level, the bodhisattva practitioner must abandon all ugly behavior. This means we must not go running around in an unattractive or disgusting manner. When we sit down, we should not sit down heavily or collapse in our chair but sit in a proper manner. When we sit in meditation, we must not extend our legs out in a disrespectful manner or have any sort of physical bearing which is sloppy or unattractive. In short, the body must be used properly and in a wholesome and mindful manner, creating a pleasing appearance.

When speaking, the bodhisattva practitioner must do so in a gentle and meaningful manner, not speaking at length unnecessarily and avoiding harsh or hurtful talk. The proper behavior of speech involves using the speech in a virtuous manner, to recite mantras and sutras, to give teachings, and to speak whenever it is appropriate to benefit another being.

On a mental level, the bodhisattva practitioner must abandon any thoughts which spring from pursuit of acquisitions and honor. The mental attitude which desires acquisition of honor is the attitude which gives rise to all of the unwholesome and afflicted activities. We become greedy and caught up in webs of illusion. In regard to this it is taught in a sutra that acquisitions and honors are just like drinking water in a dream. If we are thirsty in our sleep and dream that we drink water, no matter how much water we drink, we will never be satisfied. In the same way, when we pursue acquisitions and honors in everyday life, no matter how much we obtain, we will never be satisfied because of their illusionary quality.

The pure mental attitude which we must cultivate once we have abandoned the impure activities is outlined in thirteen sections of ethics and morals described in the *Bodhisattvabhumi* by Asanga. The obligations are first, to aid and assist whoever is sincerely practicing the dharma; second, to clear away the miseries of all living beings, specifically those which arise from the afflicted emotional states; and third, to teach the method of cutting off and stopping those afflicted mental states which give rise to misery.

The fourth obligation is to remember the kindness of living beings in this and former lifetimes, and act accordingly to repay this kindness; fifth, to protect living beings who are beset and tormented by fears; and sixth, to relieve miseries of living beings whenever we see them occurring.

The seventh obligation is to give away any material possessions we have if we see that another living being is in need of them, and eighth is to properly teach the dharma to any who are in need of teaching. It is unethical to hold the dharma as our own possession or be stingy with it. The moment we see a being that is in need of the teaching, we must give it to the best of our ability.

The ninth obligation is to relieve the minds of living beings through counseling and teaching. For instance, if someone is suffering from some great pain in their leg and they are feeling miserable about it, the bodhisattva must find some way to relieve their minds and make them happy by taking away the mental burden. One way of doing this might be to instruct the sick person that the pain they now have is the ripened effect of their bad karma which is manifesting itself in this illness. They should rejoice that it is being exhausted in this way. They can turn this common, depressing pain into a practice of great compassion by making a prayer that all the miseries of living beings will be relieved by being gathered into this pain. This counsel to take upon themselves the mental miseries of all other living beings will negate their own small sense of dissatisfaction.

When we contemplate and understand this teaching, we see it is indeed a method of transforming our troubles into great benefit. Instead of feeling sorry for ourselves when we are sick or in pain, and having not only this physical pain but also the great mental anguish of feeling that our precious possession, our body, has some difficulty, we can transmute that pain into a wish to take away from living beings all their miseries. Our minds become relieved of our own small difficulties and we also transform this misery into the benefits which arise from bodhisattva conduct.

The tenth obligation is to bring joy to others. The bodhisattva fulfills others by the body quality of being gentle, the speech quality of being inspiring, and the mind qualities of being stable, profound, and undistracted by worldly consideration.

The eleventh obligation is to properly subdue beings. The bodhisattva is not only obligated to be gentle, kind, and generous but must also be wrathful if a situation calls for it. The bodhisattva must subdue those who are in need of being subdued, that is, those who are acting in an improper way which is harmful to themselves or others. The bodhisattva must subdue them with whatever powerful means are available and convert them to acting properly.

The twelfth obligation is to manifest miraculous activities, especially to frighten living beings who are unable to be subdued by any other method. Both wrathful and miraculous activities are used to make living beings stop any sort of nonvirtuous activity and are only employed by advanced bodhisattvas since such great skill is required to properly perceive the need and carry out the action. At times a teacher will have a disciple who will have studied a certain amount and will, without deep understanding, feel they have learned everything they can from this teacher. Through arrogance they will show a lack of respect to their teacher. The bodhisattva must manifest some miraculous activity to subdue such a proud disciple. When a disciple or any other being resents the good deeds of another and seeks to prevent someone else from practicing the dharma or some virtuous deed, they are embarking on a path which leads to lower existences. The bodhisattva is obligated to awaken such a being by exhibiting either some wrathful or miraculous manifestation, leading them back to virtuous activity by destroying their arrogance or jealousy. Bodhisattvas are never allowed to merely ignore these arrogant and jealous beings, saying, "Well, it is their karma," but must do everything they can to cut off the unwholesome activities. Failing to do so degenerates the Bodhisattva Vow.

The thirteenth and last obligation is to generate faith and devotion in living beings by expressing the aspiration to perfect Buddhahood, by praising the spiritual teachers who enable us to approach it, and by expressing the virtues of the Buddha, Dharma, and Sangha. This concludes the thirteen sections of ethics and manners which benefit living beings.

The *increase of ethics and morals* has the same three components as the increase of generosity. Through pure insight, ethics and morals become greater; through wisdom, ethics and morals become very extensive; and finally through dedication, ethics and morals become limitless.

The *purification of ethics and morals* is identical to the purification of generosity. First, through the realization of shunyata, the practice of ethics and morals does not become a cause of or engagement in samsara. Second, when ethics and morals are practiced through a sense of compassion for living beings, the practices do not engage in or lead to involvement with the Hinayana Path.

The *results of the practice of ethics and morals* has two divisions, the ultimate and the temporary. The ultimate effect is the attainment of perfect Buddhahood. The temporary result is that even though we may have no desire for it, we will have happy and harmonious conditions in this lifetime. The usual pattern is that those who gain great enjoyments, pleasant surroundings, and desirable possessions will fall into a preoccupation with them, which slows any spiritual progress and causes these people to fall again into samsaric activities. However, those who guard their ethics and morals will not lose their spiritual progress or become remiss in their spiritual activities, no matter how great their possessions become.

The final temporary result of practicing ethics and morals is that we will obtain again and again the perfect human rebirth, endowed with leisure and opportunity and all of the necessary prerequisites for dharma practice. In this way, we will continue to have an unobstructed path until we attain the ultimate state of Buddhahood.

Questions

In the process of earning a living we have to acquire things and I'm not sure how to reconcile this with the obligation not to seek acquisitions.

Acquisitions will come to us naturally when we practice ethics and morals, and when they come to us without our seeking them, then this becomes an additional help to our practice of benefiting beings. The problem with acquisitions is if they become our objective so that we seek them at all costs. This state of mind becomes the source of all kinds of difficulties and bad attitudes which harm ourselves and others. The attitude of desiring very strongly is to be avoided.

In regards to the bodhisattva having an obligation to help those in need and not to just say, "Oh, that's their karma," how do you decide who you should help? There are many people starving to death in Calcutta and many people being mugged and killed in this country, but there are only twenty-four hours in a day and we have a limit to our energy. How do we choose the ones to help?

First of all, in Buddhist teachings it is the mind which attains Buddhahood. We seek with our minds how to do the most good. If someone appears before you who you can immediately help, then you should do so. However, if you tried to help the starving people in Calcutta, you might not have enough money. If you got all your money together, maybe you could buy a ticket to India and make it to Calcutta. You would be on the street with no money and the best you could do is look at the starving people. And then what are you going to do? It is better to contemplate before we do these things. In the case of someone far away, we should definitely not abandon them in our thoughts. We can make a real prayer from our hearts that by the blessing of the Three Jewels their miseries are relieved and that we obtain some power so that in the future we really can benefit them.

When we think of the killing and mugging in this country, we must extend our minds and use this situation as an object of contemplation and prayer. We may pray that these people be freed of the afflictions which lead them to kill one another and pray for the blessings of the Three Jewels. If you were to just run out into the street and jump between these fighting people and try to stop them from killing each other, you might be killed yourself and in the process lose your precious human opportunity. In the end you would be very angry and from your anger you would be reborn in lower states. So it is better to stop and think before you act, so that you can choose the best way to help beings.

I have two questions. How can I relieve the mental sufferings of others when I'm not sure I can recognize them? And can you talk more on receiving ethics and morals from those who possess them?

It is difficult to understand the mental troubles of other beings in the beginning. What we have to do is look into our own minds and understand our own mental difficulties, our own mental sufferings, and then we can begin to understand the miseries of other living beings. As far as relieving these miseries, it is not easy. It is not in our power to relieve the mental miseries of others in a true or ultimate sense; only the Buddha, Dharma, and Sangha have that ability. Our situation is compared to a mother who has no arms. If that mother's child falls into a fire, the mother urgently wants to pull the child out but has no arms and is unable to do it. In the same way, we lack the ability to relieve the mental anguish of others in the ultimate sense. But, just as that mother can call to someone else for help, so we can pray to the Buddha, Dharma, and the Sangha that they relieve the miseries of other beings. If we make this prayer from a very deep and thorough sense of faith and devotion, then it will directly help living beings.

What is meant by properly taking the vows of ethics and morals from another is that it is not enough for us to set a certain pattern of ethics and manners for ourselves. If we wish to practice the ethics and morals of the bodhisattva in order to attain the state of Buddhahood, then we must take the correct vows and practice the correct ethics and morals. In order to do this, they must be received from someone who possesses the lineage. The lineage from the Buddha down to the present is compared to a bridge. The Buddha resides on the other side and the lineage is the unbroken line, the bridge, of spiritual masters from the Buddha down to the present. Just like a great bridge, if it is unbroken, then we can cross over; otherwise we cannot reach our destination.

How do we find the balance between too strict a moral discipline, where you are so watchful of yourself that you don't do anything spontaneously, and too lax a moral discipline, where you create unwholesome karma for yourself?

Three types of morality are taught in the Buddhist tradition, the Pratimoksha ethics, the Bodhisattva ethics, and the Vajrayana ethics. The Pratimoksha governs the physical conduct of the body; it is extremely detailed, strict, and hard to follow. Likewise the Vajrayana is a very exacting code, requiring a very powerful urge for Buddhahood on behalf of all beings. Bodhi Mind must be joined with a clear grounding in shunyata to give one the great heart and courage necessary to practice the Vajrayana morality. The

Bodhisattva code of ethics and morals described in this chapter is a middle path between the Pratimoksha and Vajrayana and is a good one to follow.

You must remember that there is no code of ethics and morals which the Buddha taught which does not require some asserted effort and dedication. All of them require practice, devotion, and enthusiasm. For example, if you want to enjoy a cup of tea, you have to put out the effort to gather the necessary things and combine them in the proper way and wait for them to come together before you can enjoy them; so when you want the incalculable bliss of the attainment of Buddhahood, you certainly have to be willing to dedicate yourself to a certain amount of work.

The bodhisattva code has two branches, the Vow of the Enlightened Attitude and the actual Bodhisattva Vow. The Vow of the Enlightened Attitude is not a formal vow. We just commit ourselves to it. The Enlightened Attitude precedes the Bodhisattva Vow which is the move toward action. If you carefully guard the Vow of the Enlightened Attitude, the benefits are incalculable. It is like a seed which, if carefully tended, grows into a great flourishing plant. If it is not tended, there is no sin but, just like a seed, it will die. This is a very safe vow to take. With the Bodhisattva Vow, it is a little more difficult.

What happens if someone takes the Bodhisattva Vow and in their next life they are born in a place that does not have the dharma teaching?

If you take the Bodhisattva Vow in this lifetime and properly practice the bodhisattva code of ethics and morals, there will be no way that you can escape the dharma in your next life. Where you will be reborn is dependent upon your own karma.

Will you discuss wrathful actions in more detail?

Wrathful actions are not acts of anger. They have a pure motivation and can only be performed by the qualified. The bodhisattva must be helping others to pacify emotions and stopping the causes of suffering. If we are wrathful without qualification, or refuse wrathful actions if we are qualified, then we are lying. So you can see that even if we have wrathful or miraculous powers, we must abide by a standard of ethics and morals.

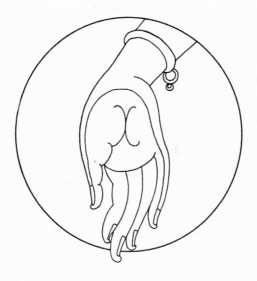

Buddha's hand represents patience.

Chapter Five
Patience

As in the previous two chapters, the paramita of patience is divided into seven parts: the detriments of not practicing and benefits of practicing patience; the nature of patience; the classifications of patience; defining characteristics; increase; purification; and results.

The *detriment of not practicing patience* is that we destroy the good effects of the virtues we have accumulated by practicing generosity and ethics and morals. Anger is the result of a lack of patience and is the mechanism or force whereby all wholesome qualities are obliterated. As the *Bodhisattvabhumi* asks, "When we part from patience and allow hatred or anger to come into our minds, what need is there to speak of making progress toward enlightenment?"

Patience is the most powerful of all the virtues. The lack of patience magnifies the effect of each transgression; the presence of patience magnifies the effect of each virtuous deed.

The *benefits of practicing patience* are that it allows us to accomplish all things that we desire in the present time and, in the future, it will allow us to attain the state of perfect Buddhahood. In the sutra *Pitaputrasamagamana*, it is taught that we exclude any possibility of practicing dharma as long as anger is in our minds; by eliminating anger and practicing patience, we open the way for our progress towards Buddhahood.

The *nature of patience* is concerned with our motivation for practicing this paramita. If we practice patience with the idea that we will become known as a very patient person, this is not very good. If we refrain from anger because we are afraid people won't like us, this is not the correct motivation. The nature of patience is that we can accept any harm done to us or any difficult situation without getting angry because we feel a sense of compassion toward the living beings involved.

There are three *classifications of patience:* the patience which accepts the harm done to us by another; the patience which accepts misery at the time of engaging in virtue; and the patience in approaching the dharma.

These three types of patience are examined more closely in *defining characteristics.* The definition of the first type of patience is the mind which does not lose patience when harm is done to ourselves or those to whom we are closely attached. This harm includes physical and mental pain as well as anything which obstructs or hinders us, or those we are close to, from being happy.

The practice of this type of patience is threefold. First, we keep the mind in a calm and undisturbed state. Second, we do not return the harm done to us or to those we care for. Third, we do not hold the harm which was done to us in our minds.

Shantideva taught many skillful ways in which we can cultivate the first practice, calm thoughts. One method is to consider that the person who has done us harm was carried away by their own anger. What they did was not truly done by them because they had no power to resist the force of anger and therefore we cannot appropriately get angry with them. We should hold this in our minds so that it will immediately arise and we will not mistakenly get angry with the person.

Another perspective on this practice of patience is that of cause and effect. When we realize that whatever we experience is our own karma ripening, the results of our own deeds coming back to us, then we will know it is not truly the fault of the person causing us harm. It is our own fault that in past lives we committed the harm which is now returning to us in this form. Another aspect of this reasoning is that we can see that we have habitually done harm to others in this life and in infinite former lifetimes. When one being comes to us now and harms us in some way, this is merely one instance of harm being returned to us, and how can we get angry when we ourselves are guilty of innumerable such acts in the past?

The next point which Shantideva makes is that by taking on this body, we are taking on the instrument whereby we are harmed. Without our own bodies, there is no way that another can hurt us. Nothing exists without dependence on something else, so there is no possibility of another being harming us unless we participate as an equal partner by providing the bodies to be harmed.

By ignorance and delusion, our minds have created this whole situation, taking on again and again these physical bodies, identifying with them and clinging to them out of delusion. When we see that our minds' own nature is very pure, that it is in fact shunyata, emptiness, then we will know that our minds cannot be harmed.

Because we have received these teachings on patience, we have an advantage. We know that others' harmful acts come out of ignorance. If we participate in harm, then we act in real ignorance. We know this will only cause us further misery, while patience will bring happiness. This knowledge should fuel our compassion for those who harm us.

The next teaching given by Shantideva is that we must see the being who harms us as actually being very kind to us. The reason that we should view them as beneficial to us is that only when we have someone who harms us do we have a reason to practice patience. Through practicing patience, we purify the infinite bad karma we have collected. Cleansing the defilements of the past allows us to accumulate vast merit which is the only way we can approach and attain Buddhahood. The basis of this sequence is the being who harms us in some way; this person is a kind of spiritual friend, so our feeling toward such a being should be one of gratitude.

Another method is to contemplate the role of the Buddha in our personal practice of patience. The Buddha is ultimately concerned with the welfare of all living beings. When a being does us some harm and we avoid returning the harm, the Buddha rejoices in our virtue. In this way, we open ourselves to receive the blessing of the Buddha; by receiving this blessing, we make rapid progress toward our goal of enlightenment.

The last of the skillful means taught by Shantideva is that if we hold in our minds the vast benefits of practicing patience, of attaining the goal of Buddhahood, and of transcending the miseries of samsara, then it is easy for us to forbear in any harmful situation.

There are also teachings in the *Bodhisattvabhumi* by Asanga which, when developed, help us to practice patience. These teachings consist of five ideas. The idea of preciousness states that when another being does us harm, we should realize this being has in former lifetimes been our own mother, father, teacher, helper, husband, or wife. In earlier times this being showed us incalculable kindness and is only harming us now out of delusion and ignorance. It is not appropriate to get angry, because their kindness has been so great that this one instance of harm is small in comparison.

The idea of the merely imputed states that when we believe a situation to be potentially harmful, we should realize that it is no more substantial than a dream or an illusion. Therefore it is foolish to get angry.

The next idea is that of impermanence. Asanga teaches that the nature of all beings is impermanent. Everything is in a state of flux and sentient beings are especially near to death. Of all the kinds of harm that can befall us, the very worst is that we can be killed. However death is the very nature of living beings; it is inescapable and always present. Answering harm with harm is therefore senseless. This being who has harmed us will very quickly die without our help; we ourselves will die soon, too, so it is senseless to worry about these small things.

The next idea is that of omnipresent misery. Suffering is the very nature of samsaric existence, unavoidable and inescapable. The essence of our practice is to clear away the misery of sentient beings, so it is totally inappropriate for us to add to the misery which is already so omnipresent.

Last is the idea of taking care of another being. Since we have taken the Bodhisattva Vow, we have transformed all living beings into our immediate family. It is our responsibility to take care of each and every living being since ultimately we are striving for their liberation. When we raise our minds to this thought, it becomes impossible for us to even contemplate harming a living being.

The second classification of patience in *defining characteristics* is the patience which accepts misery at the time of engaging in virtue. In order to attain Buddhahood, we have to practice virtue. Whatever difficulties come to us while striving toward Buddhahood should be accepted readily as they are a part of our progress. For instance, if we give up the world and take religious vows, we will have the difficulty of finding our living. If we observe a meditational retreat, we have the difficulties of heat and cold, hunger and thirst, and providing for our physical existence. Whatever virtuous activities we engage in, there will always be some difficulties. They will burn away our defilements so that we may approach our goal of Buddhahood. They are the very cause of our spiritual progress and therefore we should rejoice in them as they arise.

Practicing this classification of patience is compared to a person suffering from a great illness. To avoid loss of life, the person will seek medical treatment. Most medical treatment involves some difficulty such as having one's insides manipulated or cut out, taking bitter medicine, or refraining from foods and activities that one enjoys. But whatever adversities one undergoes in the course of medical treatment are preferable to allowing the illness to advance. In the same way, when we are practicing virtuous activity, we view facing adversity as preferable to continuing samsaric existence. In the dharma a hero is one who practices patience and thereby vanquishes the armies of samsara, the legions of the klesas, the afflicted emotions. Of course in the worldly sense, the hero is someone who kills many people in battle, but the dharma views this as someone who is only bludgeoning a corpse, since the very nature of living beings is that they are impermanent and will soon die. If we practice patience, we will become a heroic field marshal who vanquishes the hoards of samsaric activities.

The third classification of patience in *defining characteristics* is patience in approaching the dharma itself. When approaching the teachings on the emptiness of persons and phenomena, we must overcome our trepidations and doubts about our ability to obtain ultimate insight into reality. This means that we must exert confidence and belief that we will obtain this understanding of reality, and that we will cultivate the practice necessary for such awareness. In addition, this facet of patience requires that we view the perfect qualities of the Buddha, Dharma, Sangha, and great lamas of the past, and not become impatient with our own ability to achieve these same states.

The *increase of patience* has the same three components as the preceding two paramitas. Through pure insight, patience becomes greater; through wisdom, patience becomes very extensive; and finally through dedication, patience becomes limitless.

The *purification of patience* is also identical to that of the previous paramitas. Through shunyata our patience does not become a samsaric activity; and through compassion, our patience does not partake of or become a part of the Hinayana Vehicle.

The *results of patience* are twofold. The ultimate result of patience is the attainment of perfect Buddhahood. The temporary results are that we will have a long life free of illness, we will have a healthy and attractive physical body, we will be liked and respected by all beings, and we will achieve great virtue and merit.

Questions

Would you go over increase and purification again?

For the extensive teaching on those two sections, you should refer back to the first paramita of generosity.

If one begins to practice patience on the outside but becomes increasingly angry on the inside, what can one do?

This is even worse than doing nothing, for you are deceiving beings by making them think you are patient. The purpose of these teachings is not to draw any line that says that you are patient or impatient. It is presenting many ways for you to develop your mind and your practice to become more and more patient. When you look at the Buddha, you see that he wasn't always the Buddha. At one time he was a sentient being just like us. He got angry and he was impatient; gradually he purified himself, he practiced patience and became awakened. In the same way, we have to gradually purify ourselves, and these teachings are given for that purpose. If we go over these teachings again and again and begin to use them in the way Shantideva taught, we can gradually improve our practice of patience. It is important not to be discouraged if we lose patience, but try the next time to apply one of these skillful methods. In that way, we will slowly become more patient.

In the past, the great yogis and practitioners of Tibet would test their practice of patience to be sure that it was not just external. They would meditate on these teachings and make them very powerful in their own minds. Then they would leave their place of meditation and go into the towns and interact with people for the specific purpose of waiting for some harm to come to them. They would look at their own minds in that moment and practice in whatever way they could to increase their patience.

These questions are very good, but keep in mind that it is also very good to practice patience in regard to patience itself. This means that we should take the time to look at these teachings, to review them in our minds, and we will see that they do answer just about any questions we would have.

It occurs to me that anger often does not spring from aggression or hatred, but from love and concern. Is anger bad when it springs from love and concern?

The answer to your question is dependent upon knowing the mind of the angry person. If a parent is angry with their child and yells at them or slaps them, and it is done through anger or losing patience, it is bad. If it is done through compassion, because that is the only thing that will benefit the child at that time, then it is a virtuous activity. Likewise a bodhisattva is called upon at certain points, especially in the Vajrayana practice, to do very wrathful or violent activities to protect living beings. When bodhisattvas do this, their minds are motivated only by compassion for all involved.

The external activity is not as important a factor as the mind. In no case is the lack of patience a virtue. Patience is always a virtue, and anger and hatred are always non-virtuous.

Does that mean, then, that the parent could only seem to be angry, but actually be full of love?

There are quite a few different possibilities. The parents could seem to be angry and could really be compassionate, or they could seem to be angry and really be angry, or they could seem to be compassionate and could really be full of hatred and neglect. It is also very common for the parent to put on a show of being angry, out of compassion, but then the child might say or do something, and the pretended anger turns to real anger. So it is difficult to say what the motivation is, just from appearances.

There may also be the case of a very clever being who contemplates the way to do the most harm. They might decide to appear to be very compassionate in order to work their evil. This is quite common in the world of business. The whole trick is to appear concerned for the customer and all the time they are just thinking how they can get another few dollars out of this person. Of course sometimes a person who appears wrathful and impolite can be motivated by compassion and concern for others. Looking at these many examples, we can see that external appearances are ultimately of no importance in judging the true motivation for actions.

It is not appropriate to practice patience very carefully in your inner mind but then to feel free externally to hit people. The bodhisattvas who do have the power to act in a violent and wrathful way out of compassion are only those who have the ultimate insight into what benefits beings. Until we gain such high levels, we have to stick to the rules and avoid such excesses.

The practice of patience is something which must be carefully cultivated from wherever we are in our practice. We should not try to practice at a level which we are not able to sustain or have not attained at all. An example of this is the search of the great yogi Milarepa for a teacher. Meeting a Nyingma lama who was a very advanced practitioner, Milarepa said to him, "I have to obtain Buddhahood in this very lifetime, so please tell me what dharma I should practice." This lama said he taught Dzogchen and it was so powerful that one could meditate on it at night, and attain Buddhahood by daybreak. If one really had the correct karma, then without even meditating at all one could obtain Buddhahood just by hearing the teaching. Milarepa was very happy when he heard this and thought to himself, "Oh, I once learned this black magic so well that I was even able to kill many people with it. I was so good at it that I must really have this spiritual karma. I must be one of these people with the good karma who can just hear the teaching and get enlightened." So he didn't even bother to meditate; he just went to sleep. When Milarepa woke up in the morning, the lama came and said, "Well, how are you doing? Did you attain Buddhahood yet?" Milarepa said, "No, I just slept more than usual." Even though the lama spoke truly and had attained a very high level, the student Milarepa was making a very big mistake in presuming that he had reached such a high level himself that he didn't need to practice.

Can our own patience be effective in purifying another person's anger, or because of their karma will that person just continue to be angry?

When we practice patience toward someone and we do

so with the true heartfelt thought of helping, really wishing them to be relieved of their afflicted attitudes, it will indeed help to purify them, to get rid of their anger. If it is done with a really deep bodhisattva attitude, then it can have incredible significance in helping other beings. However, if we practice patience with a worldly attitude, it is of very little benefit to anyone, because we are just deceiving those around us.

Patience is an antidote for anger. Are the remaining paramitas antidotes for the other afflicted emotions?

Yes, to a degree. Patience is the antidote for anger, generosity for greed, ethics and morals for desire, and both wisdom and meditative concentration for ignorance. The afflicted emotions of pride and jealousy are not specifically related to any paramita.

You said that the Buddha rejoices in our virtue. Does that mean he is watching over us?

Buddha is not paying any particular attention to you but he is omniscient. He is sad for your sufferings and rejoices in your virtue which will end that suffering. He does not punish your bad actions. The idea of God judging us is a Western idea. Buddha is just naturally, effortlessly there, like the sun.

How do we cultivate confidence in approaching the dharma?

As a student, you build confidence through devotion and by asking for the blessings of your teacher. If your teachers have done hardship, then maybe you won't have to do the hardship because you connect with them in devotion. This is their blessing.

This may sound silly, but it seems like all this study and practice takes a long time. I heard that this was supposed to be a fast way to enlightenment. Was I wrong?

When His Holiness the Dalai Lama came here, he made a

joke about how Americans are always looking at their watches. They judge everything by minutes and seconds. Instead of thinking in terms of eons, they wish to attain Buddhahood in a few minutes, a few seconds. Americans need to learn patience. This is only a fast way to enlightenment if you work hard every minute practicing these paramitas, especially patience.

The wheel represents diligence.

Chapter Six
Diligence

The fourth perfection, diligence is divided into seven parts: the detriment of not practicing and benefits of practicing diligence; the nature of diligence; the classifications; defining characteristics; increase; purification; and the results of practicing diligence.

The **detriment of not practicing diligence** is that even though we may be generous and moral and patient, if we are not energetic and diligent in these practices, they become useless. Without diligence, no benefit will come from our efforts, as we will be unable to accomplish good and wholesome activities. If we are unable to accomplish these deeds, we are unable to help living beings and attain our goal of liberation. In the sutras the Buddha says that without diligence, all the other perfections come to nothing.

The **benefits of practicing diligence** are first, that all wholesome activities and excellent qualities will increase; second, the wholesome activities and excellent qualities will not degenerate; and third, the great treasury of insight and wisdom of the Buddha will be obtained.

The simile that is given at this point is that the samsaric world is like a mountain pass with a great wall of stone blocking the way. When we come up against this wall of stone, we must have diligence to overcome the obstacle. Likewise we are now confronted with the great obstacle of the world of samsara; in order to get to the other side, we need diligence. It is said that through possessing the perfection of diligence, the attainment of a perfect manifest Buddhahood becomes very accessible to us.

The **nature of diligence** is feeling pleased with striving for whatever is good and wholesome. It is further described as the antidote to laziness.

There are three types of laziness which can be remedied by the practice of diligence. First we have the type of laziness called lassitude. This is characterized by a sleepy or lethargic feeling and by a tendency to be attached to restfulness and pleasure. By the force of these feelings we become unable to accomplish virtue. In one of the sutras, the Buddha is addressing a gathering of monks called bhikshus. He says, "Oh, bhikshus, life is very short. Your existence in this life is ephemeral. Even the teachings of the Buddha cannot last and will disappear from this world. Therefore the strenuous application of diligence is important."

Some people will say, "I understand it is necessary to accomplish virtue. However I am busy now. Before I die I will certainly accomplish virtue and practice diligently." It is said in the *Bodhicharyavatara* that this is a very foolish attitude, because the nature of our lives means that it is uncertain how long we will live. No matter what age we are, we do not know whether we will live another moment, another day, another year. If we wait to practice virtue until we are approaching death, it will be too late. The teaching is given that the Lord of Death waits for no one. We should not expect that when our times comes, we will know it beforehand, and have the opportunity to accomplish virtue or do whatever wholesome activities we had in mind. It is totally wrong to ever put off the accomplishment of the good and wholesome.

In the *Bodhicharyavatara* it says that in this life we can never be sure which comes first, the next day or the next lifetime. Therefore we should put off the worldly plans we have made for tomorrow and quickly accomplish the purposes of the next lifetime. Our attitude toward lassitude must be like our attitude toward a poisonous snake that falls into our laps. If this were to happen, most of us would not deliberate very long about tomorrow, but would set about getting rid of the snake; our attitude toward lassitude must be the same.

A similar example is given in the *Friendly Letter* of Nagarjuna. He says that our attitude toward lassitude must be like the attitude of someone whose hair has caught fire. They are not going to sit around and contemplate what they are going to fix for dinner or where they are going to go the next day. They will quickly put out the fire in whatever way they can. This is the attitude we must cultivate toward this first kind of laziness.

The second type of laziness is mental lethargy. This way of thinking leads us to say, "Oh I am just an insignificant, helpless being who is very attached to worldly things and who has done many unwholesome activities. The attainment of Buddhahood is so far away that there is no use in even thinking about it. I do not have the wisdom or the ability even to lead my own life properly, not to speak of helping other beings. Why bother to think of attaining Buddhahood?"

To counteract this lethargy, we can contemplate other beings. Even an ant or a worm can attain Buddhahood through the practice of diligence. Any being can be a bodhisattva. When we realize this and contemplate it in our hearts, it is no longer difficult to have great confidence. We who have obtained this precious human existence and have met the teachings of the Buddha, have the opportunity to practice them. We can be very confident that Buddhahood is something which we can quickly attain if we are energetic in our practice.

The third type of laziness is gross laziness. This is when we devote ourselves to such things as subduing our enemies in the world, chasing after and holding onto friends and loved ones, and working to accumulate wealth and possessions. To overcome this type of laziness we need to understand that to engage in worldly activities becomes the source of great misery for ourselves and is a total distraction from what is good and wholesome. If we persist, we will waste this lifetime and suffer the future consequences of having made no progress toward liberation.

There are three *classifications of diligence:* the diligence of armor; the diligence of application; and the diligence of not being satisfied. The first leads to strong motivation, the second to strong application, and the third to the completion of both.

The *defining characteristics* of the diligence of armor are that diligence protects the mind and that it is unlimited. Usually when we put on a suit of armor, it protects the body. In this case the armor is put on the mind to protect it. The armor is like a pledge, which we take to heart and to the deepest part of our minds, that from this moment on until the moment when the last living being has been freed from misery, we will practice with diligence.

In one sutra which dealt with this topic, the Buddha stated that the diligence of armor must be incalculable. The reason for this is that living beings themselves are unfathomable in number, so the resolve to benefit them must likewise be without limit. We cannot say that we will practice diligently for a few years or even a few eons and then take a rest. We must think that from this moment on, as long as there are living beings in samsara, we will wear this armor of diligence.

In the *Bodhisattvabhumi* it is stated that the bodhissattva does not consider the misery of any being insignificant. If it will relieve the misery of even one living being, the bodhisattva who has diligence is happy to spend an eon of time in the lowest pit of hell.

The *defining characteristics* of the diligence of application are threefold: the diligence which eradicates the afflicted attitudes; the diligence which accomplishes virtue; and the diligence which works for the benefit of all living beings.

To practice the diligence of application which eradicates the afflicted emotions, we begin by contemplating those emotions. Realizing that these mental patterns are the source and foundation of samsara and our misery, we then seek untiringly and energetically to dispel them.

The diligence which dispels the afflicted emotions is like the great lion who is king of the jungle. He sits in the middle of the jungle and whatever other wild animals exist there, dogs, jackels, or small cats, come and go without disturbing him. Although they might wish to take his place or attack him, they are afraid to do so. He sits majestically in the center of the jungle, totally at ease and without fear. This lion is like our minds when we practice diligently. The various animals are like the afflicted emotions. When they arise they do not disturb us. Our mind is tranquil in the face of whatever feelings, activities, or thoughts occur.

There is another teaching which compares the afflicted states to a vessel that is filled to the brim with oil. We must carry this vessel a certain distance and the problem is that there is a huge person on guard with a giant sword raised over our heads. We are told that if we should lose one single drop of oil, this sword will immediately descend and chop off our heads. In this situation, we would guard the oil diligently and carry it carefully without spilling it. This is the diligence we must have toward our minds which is like a vessel. We should not allow even one tiny drop of affliction to enter into it.

The second type of diligence of application is that which accomplishes virtue. This is the diligence which is applied to all the other activities on the Bodhisattva Path, specifically the other five of the Six Paramitas. This diligence itself has five aspects, the first of which is called the continual practice of diligence. This states that the practice of diligence must not be an occasional activity to be worked at for a while and then abandoned. On the contrary, it must be resolved that from this moment until the perfection of Buddhahood, we will not waiver in our diligence.

The second aspect of the diligence which accomplishes virtue is called devoted diligence. This means that we are totally devoted to practicing all the activities of the Six Perfections. Whatever obstacles arise, we are not for one moment discouraged by them.

The third aspect of the diligence which accomplishes virtue is unwaivering diligence. In working toward the accomplishment of the activities involved in the perfections, we do not waiver or become distracted by any type of afflicted emotion.

The fourth aspect of the diligence which accomplishes virtue is the diligence which does not turn back. In practicing the activities of the Six Perfections, we do not turn back because of attacks or abuse.

The final aspect of the diligence which accomplishes virtue is the diligence which is free of arrogance. If we practice the paramita of diligence, the natural result is that our good qualities and spiritual accomplishments increase. If we become arrogant or proud because of this, our diligence becomes worldly rather than spiritual. We must be careful to guard against this.

The diligence of application which benefits living beings involves the practice of the Six Perfections. Whatever is necessary to benefit living beings, whether mental, verbal, or physical activities, must be energetically accomplished. This means we might be required to act gently or wrathfully, to give wealth, advice, or teaching, or anything else appropriate to benefit beings.

The *defining characteristic* of the diligence which will not be satisfied is that when we are practicing the perfections and benefiting beings, we should at no point be satisfied with our activities. No matter how much virtue we do or how much merit we accumulate, we should always seek to do more until we attain the state of Buddhahood. In the *Bodhicharyavatara* it says that living beings are never satisfied in acquiring worldly desires. Even though their benefit is illusory and leads to misery, they are sought more and more. If beings are never satisfied in seeking worldly desires, how can we ever be satisifed in practicing virtue and seeking Buddhahood when the benefits are so much greater?

The *increase of diligence* has the same three components as in the former perfections. Through pure insight, diligence becomes greater; through wisdom, diligence becomes very extensive; and finally through dedication, diligence becomes limitless.

The *purification of diligence* is identical to that of the previous paramitas. Through the realization of shunyata, our diligence does not become a samsaric activity; and through compassion, our diligence does not partake of or become a part of the Hinayana Vehicle. The extensive explanation of these categories of increase and purification is to be found in the chapter on generosity.

The *results of diligence* are twofold, the ultimate and the temporary. The ultimate result is, of course, the attainment of perfect, manifest Buddhahood. The temporary results are that, through the practice of diligence, we will acquire many good qualities and have the respect and devotion of living beings. We will have a long and fortunate life and be very happy in our world. Based upon this, we will have the increased opportunity to expand our bodhisattva attitude and practice. We can then quickly attain the perfect state of Buddhahood.

Questions

The diligence of application which benefits living beings requires us to be sometimes vigorous and sometimes peaceful. With regard to people who aren't interested in dharma, who criticize it, or don't practice it, how can we tell which method to use?

Are you asking how we can be diligent in our activities to help living beings who don't understand the dharma or don't have any devotion toward it?

Yes.

As far as relating to someone's knowledge or lack of knowledge of the dharma, if you are called upon by someone who sincerely asks you to tell them about the dharma, you can easily understand their words or manner and you can decide whether it is sincere or not, and you can, to the best of your ability without being lazy or holding anything back, do your best to teach them. If you don't understand them, you can still do your best to give them what they wish; but always, no matter who it is, you have to work to benefit them in the appropriate way. You cannot seek to do vigorous activity like teaching someone vigorously or wrathfully just at random. If you go into the store and act wrathfully, someone might be wrathful right back and maybe hit you, so you have to do what is appropriate.

How can an ant or a worm attain Buddhahood?

Bodhisattvas appear in every realm. They care about all

kinds of beings, respect all beings—all life. Every living being could be a bodhisattva. That is why, in these teachings, we talk about benefiting "living beings" rather than just "human beings." Bodhisattvas plant the seed of the dharma in ants and all beings. After the ant's present karma is exhausted, it may act in another life from that seed of dharma, taking another step toward enlightenment.

A bodhisattva doesn't have to have the form of an ant or worm to plant the seed of dharma in those beings. The high lamas, for instance, will use everything around them to help all beings. They constantly say mantras for all beings to hear, they purchase incarcerated animals about to die and set them free,they make stupas out of their food and frequently give away all their possessions. This stainless pure motivation connects with every living being. If you have ever met a high lama or other bodhisattva, you know how immediately they affect you. Animals and other beings feel this, too.

It seems like there are so many things to do to reach enlightenment. Couldn't we just go into retreat and say mantras? It would be easier than having to accomplish Buddhahood when we are surrounded by people.

We will say more about retreat in the next chapter. Perhaps an example will help you to feel all right about how much diligence it takes to reach enlightenment. Let us say we wished for a certain pleasure, perhaps the simple pleasure of a cup of tea. We would need the stove, the fuel for the stove, the pot, and the water; we would also need tea, milk, sugar, and lemon. Even if we have all these things, we have to gather them together and then we have to apply some energy. It will take effort to put the water in the pan, turn on the stove or light the fire, wait for the water to boil, put the tea in the pot and wait for it to steep, get the milk and put it in, combine it all and finally put it in the cup.

Then we can drink it and we can get some of this feeling of enjoyment, of pleasure. This is a very small illustration. What we seek is not just the momentary or ephemeral pleasure of a cup of tea, but the cosmic pleasure of the attainment of perfect Buddhahood, in which we have transcended all miseries and attained perfect lasting peace and happiness. We should understand that this might take a little effort also.

The mala represents meditative concentration.

Chapter Seven
Meditative Concentration

We enter into the explanation of meditative concentration by listing its seven topics: the detriments of not practicing and benefits of practicing meditative concentration; the nature of meditative concentration; the classifications; defining characteristics; increase; purification; and results of practicing meditative concentration.

One *detriment of not practicing meditative concentration* is that although we possess the virtues of generosity, morality, patience, and diligence, if we do not have meditative concentration, our mind becomes distracted and is subject to the vicissitudes of the afflicted emotional states. Because of this, the mind is unable to abide in tranquility or happiness. Shantideva has stated that the person whose mind is distracted is at the mercy of all the afflicted mental states and by the force of them become miserable. Without samadhi, which arises from meditative concentration, there is no possibility that a sense of superknowledge can develop. Superknowledge (abhijna in Sanskrit, and ngonparshaypa, in Tibetan) means prescience, the knowledge of things or events before they happen. Without this, we are unable to know the correct way to help living beings and therefore cannot attain Bodhi Mind.

Another detriment of not practicing meditative concentration is that without it, true wisdom cannot arise.

As long as we are bound up in the craving and clinging to the desirable appearances of the material world, we have no occasion to allow our minds to come to rest and abide in the state of meditative concentration. However, once we do have meditative concentration, a **benefit of practicing** is that we gain superknowledge and thus are able to effectively do the works and activities which benefit living beings. As we can benefit living beings, we accumulate the prerequisites for the ultimate attainment of perfect Buddhahood. Another benefit is that through the possession of meditative concentration, true wisdom arises. The mental stabilization of meditation joined with true wisdom completely destroys the afflicted emotional states.

A further benefit of the possession of meditative concentration is that when we possess it and practice it, we will eventually gain the ultimate insight into the nature of reality. Having gained this insight, compassion spontaneously arises for all other beings who fail to see reality. Therefore, the possession of meditative concentration serves as the basis for truly helping all living beings attain both liberation from samsara and perfect Buddhahood.

The **nature of meditative concentration** is said to be the abiding of the mind in oneness with a sense of wholesomeness. The method whereby the mind can achieve this is dwelling in isolation. In the way that it is used here, isolation has two meanings, physical isolation and mental isolation. Physical isolation is separation from the hustle and bustle of the world. To understand physical isolation better, the conditions of both busyness and isolation will be examined.

Worldly busyness is the condition of being distracted and agitated by living beings and worldly possessions. The cause of this is our attachment to living beings, family, friends, and enemies, and our attachment to wealth, possessions, power, influence, fame, and praise. The evils of this condition are that our body, speech, and mind remain distracted and unable to do virtuous deeds. Beyond this, we are distracted from approaching meditative concentration, samadhi, and purity of insight, all of which are necessary to attain liberation.

The condition of physical isolation makes possible the attainment of meditative concentration. The condition of physical isolation is separation from the worldly busyness and this is achieved by staying in a physically isolated retreat. The sutras describe isolated retreat as that place of meditation which is five hundred bow-lengths from the nearest settlement. The length of a bow placed end to end five hundred times is said to be the limit of our ability to hear a human being who yells as loud as they can.

The virtue of practicing such isolation is that if we take only seven steps in the direction of such an isolated retreat with the pure intent to relieve the misery of all beings, the merit of these seven steps is greater than if we were to offer to the Buddha all the desirable and excellent objects of this and other worlds. The further value of staying in such an isolated retreat is that we overcome the afflicted emotions and abandon any concern with what is called the Eight Worldly Dharmas of gain and loss, pleasure and unhappiness, praise, blame, fame, and disgrace. In addition, we attain both meditative equanimity (Skt: shamata) and pure insight (Skt: vipasyana).

In examining the nature of meditative concentration, we come to the second method whereby the mind may abide in oneness with wholesomeness, the method of mental isolation. This aspect of isolation means separation from the tendency toward dualistic conceptualized thinking. Once we have set ourselves apart in physical retreat, we will sit down and examine our situation. Contemplating our fear of endless wandering in samsara, and our intense misery and the ceaseless pain caused by our attachment to the world, we develop the very deepest sense of aversion toward samsara.

Having developed this sense of revulsion we realize that we have come to this retreat to attain liberation and to help other beings. The question arises, "Now that I am here, what should I do to attain this goal? What should I do with my physical body?" If we fight with other beings, kill animals, steal, or commit various sexual activities, then these actions would be the source of further misery. If we engage in such activities, we are acting exactly like wild animals in the vicinity. Even if we are isolated, we would obtain no benefits from such a retreat. Instead, our physcial bodies must be disciplined and avoid all these unwholesome activities.

Next we ask ourselves, "Now that I am in retreat, what should I do with my power of speech?" If we talk about whatever comes to mind, speaking of worldly things, we would be just like the birds in the forest chattering away and would certainly not accomplish anything beneficial. Realizing that we have great nonvirtue from speaking senselessly or casually about unimportant things, we must abandon these actions and engage only in the wholesome use of the power of speech, such as reciting mantras or sutras.

Examining our mind we ask ourselves, "What should I do in this retreat with my mind? Should I think about worldly things and engage in the emotions of anger, jealousy, desire, pride, and greed?" When we contemplate this, we realize that it would be senseless for the very reason that we have come into retreat to leave such things behind. We would be no different than the wild animals in the vicinity whose thoughts are filled with desire and anger. By completely clearing such thoughts from our minds, we can use our minds to accomplish the stabilization of the mind and attain the state of liberation. These, then, are the steps whereby we free our minds from the dualistic thought constructions which are the usual source of distraction for our minds.

By isolating the body from worldly busyness and isolating the mind from dualistic thought constructions, mental concentration and stabilization naturally arise. It is not something that must be constructed or in some way fabricated; it will spontaneously and naturally arise when the mind and body have been freed from worldly concerns. So this is the general method of obtaining isolation.

Part of the nature of meditative concentration is that, in practicing it, we encounter its enemies. The specific enemies of meditative concentration are the klesas, the afflicted emotions. There are five of these and each has a specific antidote which is applied whenever they arise while we are practicing meditative concentration. If one of these five is the predominate source of our problem, we meditate on the specific antidote. If, on the other hand, all five are more or less equal in force, we use the sixth antidote which subdues them all.

First there is the emotion of sensual desire. Here in its strongest form is our attachment and clinging to our physical sensations, and these are centered upon our own physical body. The antidote to this is to visualize what happens to the body after death. The rigidity, rotting, stench, and disintegration that occur in the first few days are followed by putrifying and the body being eaten by worms. When we realize that our own body, to which we are so attached, is no different than a decaying corpse in its nature, we will lessen the grip of attachment. Visualizing corpses, we begin to think how each of them was associated with a person who was as attached to their body as we are to ours. But no matter how much they clung to it, no matter how much they wanted it and cherished it, in the end it came to this disgusting state. In the end, their attachment to it not only came to nothing, but was also no benefit whatsoever and a source of extreme and unbearable misery.

We will all have to come to this state of parting with the physical body. If we have been extremely attached to it, we will take rebirth as a hungry ghost, which is an existence of incredible and ceaseless misery. If we can free ourselves from attachment to our own body, the basis of all sensual desire, we naturally will have no problems with sensual attraction to anything else in the world.

Next we have the emotion of hatred. The antidote is the cultivation of loving kindness and this starts with contemplation of our dear mother who brought us into the world and nursed us and cherished us and raised us and taught us and whose kindnesses cannot be enumerated or fathomed. Thinking in this way, we cultivate a sense of cherishing, of loving. When we are able to feel this way toward our own mothers, then we extend it to our brothers and sisters and friends, to all we know and beyond that to everyone in our own country, to everyone in our own world, and finally to all beings in all directions of space.

Next we have the emotion of delusion. The antidote is contemplation of the Law of Interdependent Origination and this has two applications. One is to the world, the physical universe, and the other is to nirvana.

The worldly application of the Law of Interdependent Origination has two aspects, the causes, which are described as a twelvefold chain, and the conditions or elements. What is described by the twelvefold chain is the total interpenetration and connection of the different aspects of the world. This chain is a circle of events with no beginning, but we will start with "ignorance." This inherent ignorance is defined as not knowing anything, not realizing the mind to be Buddha Mind, or having obstacles to Buddha nature. Upon that ignorance what arises is "perception."

When this perception or conceptualization takes place, it can tend either toward the virtuous or the nonvirtuous because it is based upon ignorance; it does not know which way to go.

From having perceptions, "consciousness" arises. This is defined as a sense of knowing and leads to the activities which achieve entrance into the womb. The conjunction of the sperm and egg into an embryo are called "name and form." In the embryo, name and form will develop a physical body endowed with five physical senses. This link in the chain is called the "attainment of the senses."

When one has consciousness and senses, then there can be "contact" with objects. The consciousness contacts objects through the sense power. When contact is established, "feeling" can arise. This may be the feeling of happiness, unhappiness, or indifference.

ut of the arising of feeling comes the development of attachment to things or "desire." If it is strong enough, it leads to the next link which is the actual reaching out or "grasping" the object. This grasping leads to activity by the body, speech, and mind which is called "manifest existence."

When one has secured manifest existence, then one takes physical "birth." What necessarily arises out of the acquisition of birth is "old age and death." This completes the twelvefold chain.

This is a brief description of the chain as it applies to this condition of taking birth as a living being. In other realms, the chain is very different, since these beings are not born from a womb.

There are three divisions of these twelve links. The first is the division of the klesas or afflicted emotions and this contains three of the twelve links, ignorance, desire, and grasping. The second division is that of karma or activities, and this comprises two, perception and manifest existence.

The remaining seven form the third division, misery. In this division are consciousness, name and form, attainment of the senses, contact, feeling, birth, and old age and death.

We might compare ignorance to a farmer, karma to the field of the farmer, and consciousness to the seed which will be planted. This field is watered by desire, and the sprouts will be name and form. The remaining seven links are compared to the leaves and fruit of the plants which then arise.

We must understand that the links are in no way separate, nor do they independently think, "I, as ignorance will produce perception," or, "I, as karma, arose out of consciousness and will produce name and form." Where one exists, the others spontaneously or naturally follow. Understanding the interconnection of these links is an antidote to our basic delusion. This concludes the examination of the twelvefold chain which is the progression of causes in the worldly application of the Law of Interdependent Origination.

The conditions of the worldly application of the Law of Interdependent Origination describe the elements of our existence. The first element is earth and it is what makes our physical bodies solid. The liquid element is what causes our bodies to adhere and function within themselves. The element of heat allows our bodies to metabolize nutrients. The element of air is responsible for the flow of energy in our bodies, in particular our breathing. The element of ether or space forms our bodily cavities and the openings to our bodies. The final element is that of consciousness which is the source of all aspects of consciousness in our present bodies and the source of all the afflicted emotions.

These six elements come together to form our mental and physical being and they condition our existence. The twelvefold chain describes the genesis of our mental and physical constituents; the elements are what conditions this existence.

In the beginning of our examination of the Law of Interdependent Origination as an antidote to delusion, it was stated that there are two forms of this law, that which leads to the world, and that which leads to nirvana. We have finished examining the Law as it describes the cycle of samsara, worldly life. We now turn our attention to the nirvanic application. This requires transformation of the twelvefold chain by doing away with the primordial, basic ignorance which is the first of the twelve links. The way that ignorance is destroyed is through realizing the nonsubstantial, illusory nature of inner and outer phenomena, in other words, realizing shunyata (Tib: tong pa nyi). When ignorance is destroyed, it does not produce the condition of perception; without perception, consciousness cannot arise, and so forth. Therefore the twelvefold chain cannot occur, and one is therefore freed from samsara and obtains its transcendence. This is called the Interdependent Origination of Nirvana, and it concludes this explanation of the antidote to the afflicted state of delusion.

Delusion is the third of five basic afflictions which must be overcome, as they are obstacles to meditative concentration. The fourth of these basic afflictive states is jealousy, and the antidote is to view ourselves and others as equal. The way to do this is to contemplate that, just precisely as I myself desire happiness and peace and dislike unhappiness and trouble, so does every other living being of every variety. We all are precisely equal in this way, and there is no reason for favoring one above another.

The fifth of these afflicted states is arrogance and its antidote is the substitution of others for ourselves. It is taught that all ordinary beings in the universe cherish themselves above others, and therefore continue to take rebirth after rebirth and experience the unbearable misery of samsara. The Buddha, on the other hand, is the one who forgets about himself and cherishes each and every being, working ceaselessly for the benefit of all. He therefore attains transcendence of samsara and benefits all living beings. Realizing that these differing results come from differing actions, we see that we must abandon cherishing ourselves, replacing it with concern for others, and abandon neglecting others, replacing it with neglect of ourselves. In this way, arrogance is abandoned when we begin to see cherishing ourselves as a fault and cherishing others as a virtue. This is the last of the specific antidotes for the five afflicted emotions.

When all the afflicted emotions arise more or less equally, the antidote is the concentration upon our own breathing. In meditation, we can focus on the inhalation, the exhalation, and the pause between the two when we hold the breath. We can also count the breaths. When we focus our minds upon this process of breathing, then none of the afflicted attitudes are given a chance to arise.

In the Vajrayana there are methods to handle the arising of the afflicted mental states without suppressing them, but instead, transforming them. This is a very subtle and powerful teaching; in order to gain it and use it effectively, we must depend upon the direct teachings of our lama and the lineage of Marpa and Milarepa. It is also taught in the Six Yogas of Naropa. This concludes the teachings of the nature of meditative concentration.

The *classifications of meditative concentration* are the meditative stabilization which is the basis of a pleasant or prosperous life, the meditative stabilization which accomplishes good qualities, and the meditative stabilization which accomplishes the benefit of others.

There are five *defining characteristics* of the meditative concentration which is the basis of a pleasant or prosperous life. First, through meditative concentration we become free of dualistic thought constructions and abide in a state of wholeness or oneness. Second, through the practice of meditative concentration we burn up and consume the defilements of evil or unwholesome actions done in the past by body, speech, and mind. Through clearing them away, we attain the purity and fitness of both body and mind. Third, through meditative concentration we stop the flow of the afflictive mental states and abide in peace and tranquility. The afflicted emotions are compared to waves disturbing the surface of a lake. When the water is calm, the waves die down. If the mind stays calmly in isolation, the waves of the afflicted emotions die down, and then one can abide in peace and tranquility.

Fourth, through meditative concentration we are not disturbed by pride in our accomplishments of the different states of samadhi. Fifth, through meditative concentration we no longer differentiate between the levels of samadhi. When we reach the first level, we say, "Oh, I've attained samadhi and I feel very happy about it." At the second level, we do not stop to think that we have attained anything but we do feel happiness. At the third level, there is no longer gross happiness, but there is a subtle feeling of joy. Then at the final level, there is only the completely tranquil feeling of equanimity. At this point, we no longer differentiate between levels of samadhi.

The *defining characteristics* of the meditative concentration which accomplishes good qualities has two forms, common and uncommon. The common good qualities are those which are common to the Hinayana practice and can be obtained by the Shravakas and Pratyeka Buddhas. These are healthy long life, clairvoyance, a clear mind, and miraculous powers. The uncommon or exclusive attainments are great powers of meditative concentration which are beyond the reach of those who practice the Lesser Vehicle. Such beings do not even hear the names of these great powers and accomplishments, let alone obtain them.

The *defining characteristic* of the meditative concentration which accomplishes the purposes of others is that through meditative concentration we attain tranquility and insight. Once we have attained prescience, we know the way of actually and truly benefiting living beings, and are able to move from benefiting a few to the limitless benefit of all living beings through this knowledge. Once we have attained tranquility of meditative stabilization (Skt: shamata and Tib: sheenay) by letting the mind abide within its own essence, we can achieve insight. Insight (Skt: vipasyana and Tib: lhatong) into reality is the recognition that reality is nondual. The achievement of these two means that we will have the true ability to help living beings.

The *increase of meditative concentration* has the same three components as the former paramitas. Through pure insight, meditative concentration becomes greater; through wisdom, meditative concentration becomes very extensive; through dedication, meditative concentration becomes limitless.

The *purification of meditative concentration* is identical to that of the previous paramitas. Through the realization of shunyata, our meditative concentration does not become a samsaric activity; through compassion, it does not become a part of the Hinayana Vehicle. The extensive explanation of these two categories is to be found in the chapter on generosity.

The *results of the practice of meditative concentration* are twofold, ultimate and temporary. The ultimate benefits are that we overcome all afflicted emotions and obtain pure insight and wisdom whereby Buddhahood will be attained. Through this, the purposes of both ourselves and other beings are achieved. The temporary results are that we are able to attain the divine bliss experience.

Questions

In the explanation of the Law of Interdependent Origination, you say we have to negate ignorance. How do you do that?

The key point is to get rid of ignorance as the ultimate source of all the miseries. The method is to contemplate this process of the twelvefold chain itself, and thereby to dispel ignorance, and in particular, the misunderstanding of reality.

The basic form our ignorance takes is clinging to the ego, and the antidote to that is compassion, being concerned with others. This way we lessen the tight grip of holding to the self. So compassion functions as the means and wisdom is hopefully growing too. Our work is to seek and practice both of these at once because they require each other. Wisdom without compassion is heartless; compassion without wisdom is foolish. From this combination comes pure insight which sees reality as it actually is, and this is the end of our ignorance.

It is difficult to say more specifically, "Do this and that and it will soon go away." There is no advice to be given, but instead the Buddha taught this method, the cultivation and development of compassion for other living beings and the growth of wisdom which is the penetrating insight into reality.

Some mothers are not as wonderful as you describe. If our own mothers didn't treat us very well, how can we have an antidote for hatred? We may hate our mothers.

It is important, first, for us to acknowledge that the actions of our mothers stem from their karma and our own. This can lessen some of the harsh blame we may feel. Secondly, contemplating our mothers can still be an antidote to hatred because even if she hit us, hated us, or gave us away, she still gave birth to us. She made us and this is very kind. Our mothers gave us the precious human opportunity in this lifetime and we should contemplate that and cherish her.

What is nirvana?

In the Hinayana, it means "arhatship," the absence of pleasure, pain, and the body. The Hinayana view the body as the source of all troubles. If they can subdue it, be rid of it, then they are in nirvana, and they think this is enlightenment. Being in this state lasts a long time because of all their virtuous actions. In the end, they do not know where they are, and the Buddha radiates light to awaken them. He does this because they have taken refuge and because of his great compassion.

In the Mahayana, nirvana is a wonderful place, but it is not the state of full enlightenment that is the supreme goal.

In the twelvefold chain, what is the difference between perception and consciousness?

Perception is just thinking about things, having ideas, any ideas. You don't know how right they are. With consciousness, you know. Here is an example of the difference. Let us say I walk up to one of you and talk about a certain place named New York City. One of you who has never been there will have many perceptions about this place as I talk. Some will be accurate and some will not. You won't know which is which. One of you who has been there will recognize what I am talking about. You know New York City. Perception without consciousness can be fanciful and foolish.

Does the twelvefold chain describe our lifetime?

It takes three lifetimes, one in a body, one conscious lifetime in the Bardo after death, and one rebirth into a second solid lifetime in a body.* These three lifetimes complete one

*Editor's Note: For more information on the conscious life in the Bardo, the reader is referred to Lama Lodö's The Bardo Teachings, KDK Publications, 1982.

cycle of the chain for all beings born from a womb, not just humans.

How long should a person stay in retreat?

The person who goes into physical isolation should ideally stay there until they are totally unaffected by any worldly things. True yogis will "test" themselves by going out into the busy world. If the world does not distract or agitate them at all, and if their minds can abide in oneness, then they have achieved the goal of their retreat.

The bow and arrow represent wisdom.

Chapter Eight
Wisdom

The sixth perfection of wisdom is divided into seven sections, the first four of which are as in the other paramitas: the detriment of not practicing and benefit of practicing wisdom; the nature of wisdom; and the classifications and defining characteristics of wisdom. The fifth section is the explanation of the meaning of wisdom, the sixth concerns the cultivation of wisdom, and the seventh describes the results of this practice.

The *detriment of not practicing wisdom* is that any practitioner or bodhisattva who has developed the first five perfections and does not cultivate and perfect wisdom will have no chance of attaining enlightenment. In one sutra it is said that just as people without eyesight are unable to find the path to the city of their choice, so the five paramitas are blind without the sight of wisdom and cannot find the way to the city of Buddhahood. The *benefit of practicing wisdom* in conjunction with the other five perfections is that one can very definitely succeed in attaining this city of enlightenment.

At this point the question naturally arises that if wisdom is so vital, can we merely perfect wisdom and attain enlightenment without the aid of the other five perfections?

159

The answer to that question is no. In the sutras it says that wisdom without the skillful means of the first five paramitas and skillful means without wisdom are each a form of bondage. Wisdom without skillful means creates a state in which we are bound to the one-sided, limited nirvana of the Shravakas and Pratyeka Buddhas. There are two kinds of practitioners of wisdom without skillful means. First are the practitioners who understand or accept no other vehicle than the Hinayana. These people, not believing in the Mahayana or Vajrayana, have confidence that their present nirvana, the state of cessation and pacification, is the ultimate one. They stay in this state for many thousands of eons without ever rising up to final liberation or falling down into samsara. They remain bound to this condition of pacification. Second are the practitioners who accept the validity of the Three Yanas but practice the Hinayana. This kind of practitioner will be bound to the condition of pacification forever and never reach final liberation.

On the other hand, skillful means without wisdom leads to bondage because there is no liberation from samsara. The person who has perfected all the skillful means and lacks wisdom will be reborn again and again in the states of men and gods, experiencing ceaseless misery which is the result of accepting samsaric birth. Having skillful means without wisdom, we are in bondage to samsara.

These two limited paths, wisdom without means or means without wisdom, are said to be paths which are praised by the devils because they are obstacles to the ultimate good. In the sutras, wisdom is compared to eyesight and skillful means to legs. If we have a destination and have good eyesight but no legs, we will never get there. Likewise, if we have legs to walk on but have no eyesight, we also will not arrive. To travel to the city of enlightenment, it is necessary to have both legs, the skillful means to accomplish the path, and eyes, the wisdom to see the way. The Mayahana can be summarized into these two principles, wisdom and skillful means.

At this time, it is natural to wonder how does wisdom come forth? Does it arise by itself? The answer is no, it does not arise by itself. The example given here is of a fire. If we wish to make a fire and have just a single piece of wood, the fire will not last very long. However, if we first accumulate a great deal of nice dry wood we will have a large hot fire which will last a long time. Even when we try to put it out, it will be difficult to do so. Just as we must gather a great deal of wood to make a roaring fire, we must gather a great deal of merit to cause inexhaustible wisdom to arise. It is by practicing the other paramitas such as generosity that we accumulate this vast amount of merit.

We can also view the wood we accumulate as the defilements which come from our negative emotional patterns. Then we can perceive wisdom as being the fire which destroys them. When we are completely cleansed by the fire of wisdom, we see the true nature of our own mind. In the *Bodhicharyavatara* it is stated that all the perfections are taught and practiced for the purpose of generating wisdom.

The *nature of wisdom* is that wisdom is the ultimate and detailed direct understanding of all of existence, all aspects of phenomena.

The three *classifications of wisdom* are taken from the commentary to the *Mahayanasutralankara* (Tib: *Do de gyan*). First is worldly wisdom, second, transcendental wisdom of the lesser variety, and third, transcendental wisdom of the higher variety.

The *defining characteristic* of worldly wisdom is having some understanding of such categories as healing or medicine, logic, grammar and poetics, and manufacturing or engineering.

The two remaining classifications differ from worldly wisdom. They comprise "inner wisdom," the teachings of the Buddha. The first of these two inner wisdoms, transcendental wisdom of the lesser variety, is anything which comes under the heading of the teachings and practices of the Shravaka and Pratyeka Buddhas. These are the teachings of the Hinayana Path which are the profound understanding of the skandhas or psychosomatic constituents of individual beings. The Hinayana wisdom refutes samsara by citing the four qualities of our existence: we are bodily impure, unsatisfied, impermanent, and egoless.

The second inner wisdom, transcendental wisdom of the greater variety, comes from the study and practice of the Mahayana teachings. These seek the Hinayana goal of egolessness of personality and add to it the Mahayana understanding of the ultimate emptiness of all inner and outer phenomena.

The **explanation of the perfection of wisdom** is a clarification of the transcendental wisdom of the greater variety and is divided into six sections: the refutation of the belief in substantial existence, the refutation of the belief in nonexistence, the explanation of the fallacy of holding to the belief in nonexistence, the refutation of belief in both existence and nonexistence, the explanation of the path of liberation, and the explanation of the essence of liberation which is nirvana.

The first argument refuting the belief in substantial existence comes from the *Lam Rim* teachings and examines the faults of the belief in the two types of selfhood. It states that all belief in substantial existence is based upon holding to one of two types of ego, the subjective ego of personality and the objective ego of phenomena. This is refuted by showing the empty nature of both types of ego.

The subjective ego of personality is defined as that sense of "I" which arises out of the five psychosomatic constituents of existence (form, feeling, perception, intention, and consciousness) and their constantly changing nature. They are the basis of our clinging to the idea of subject. From the base of psychosomatic constituents of existence there arises the idea of self to which we give the name "mine;" from that there arises the dichotomy or dualism of self and other. We can say that all miseries and all unhappiness have their source in this sense of self, of "mine." The second type of ego, the objective ego of phenomena, is defined as clinging to a belief in the existence of a subjective mind and an objective world. In other words, the second type of ego is grasping onto the existence of this dualism of subject and object, of self and other. The way that the belief in these two types of ego is refuted is by demonstrating their emptiness. First we will probe the existence or nonexistence of the subjective ego.

The teacher Nagarjuna in the *Ratnavali* (Tib: *Rinchen trengwa*) said that when we look for the actual nature of the subjective ego, we will find nothing there. In other words, when we see reality we should be able to find the subjective ego, but this is not the case. When reality is seen with true knowledge, dualism does not exist. If the self were an actual separate entity, we should be able to prove its existence. There are four ways it might arise.

First, the subjective ego could arise from itself or by itself; second, it could arise from something external to itself; third, it could arise by some combination of itself and other; or fourth, it could arise from the three different times of past, present, and future. When investigating how the ego might arise from itself, we see that before it arises, either it exists or it does not exist. If it does not exist before it arises, then there is no cause whereby it can come into existence. If it does exist before it arises, then there is no need for it to arise. So in this way, the arising from itself is refuted.

Employing the same analysis, the arising of subjective ego by the power of something external can be refuted. Before an ego can arise from something external, something external must either exist or not exist. If something external does not exist, it cannot cause the ego. In fact this external object cannot exist because there is no self to cause it to arise. However, if something external does exist there would be no need for the ego to arise.

The third way that the subjective ego might arise, through a combination of itself and something external, is easily refuted. Since we have seen that ego cannot arise from itself alone nor from something external to it, we logically conclude that a combination of these two would not make the arising of subjective ego any more possible.

The fourth way that subjective ego might come into existence is through the force of the three times. However, the past cannot produce anything because the past is defined as that which is already finished. It is like the ruined seed of some plant which cannot produce any sprout. The future is something which has not come into existence yet. It is like the son of a barren woman and cannot produce anything. The present cannot produce anything by itself alone, because this would be "cause" without "effect." The present without the future can produce nothing.

The refutation of the subjective ego continues by showing that it has no place of existence in the body, the mind, or the name. Thus it has no place from which to arise. If we look at the body as the basis of the ego, we see that it is composed of several physical elements, solid, liquid, warm, and mobile. In none of these can we find the ego.

If we look to the mind as the basis for the ego, we see that the mind itself cannot be found. We do not know its location or its shape. Therefore, it cannot serve as the basis of the ego.

If we look to the name as a basis for the existence of the ego, we find that a name is just applied or designated. It has no substantial existence and therefore cannot serve as the basis for the ego. So in these examinations, we have found that the subjective ego cannot arise, nor does it exist anywhere.

Now we will explore the existence or nonexistence of the objective ego. This is done by examining the two aspects of the objective ego, the external phenomena which are grasped and the internal mind which is the grasper. Both of these are shown to be substantially nonexistent. First we will look at external phenomena.

Some schools of thought say that external phenomena substantially exist because they are built upon the conglomeration of what is called dultren in Tibetan, meaning the minutest subatomic particles. These are brought together and organized into gross matter which then form substantially existent external phenomena. To verify the existence of external phenomena requires that we examine these subatomic particles to see if the ultimate particle is divisible or not. We find that every particle has sides like east, west, north, south, top, and bottom, so even the smallest particle can be divided into six parts. If it can no longer stand as a unity because it has constituent parts, then it is not a substantially existent phenomenon.

If we deny that the subatomic particle can be divided into various parts and insist that the particle, being a unity, cannot be separated from the rest of existence, this would mean that all existence was identical and we can observe that this is not so.

We must conclude that the basis for the substantial existence of objective phenomena is refuted since the smallest particle of phenomena, the subatomic particle, can either be further divided or is found not to be the single basis of all phenomena.

Now, we ask ourselves, "What is it that we see all around us, the trees and the houses and everything else? How can we see things if they are not substantially existent?" The answer lies in examining the way in which our own minds see substantial nature in that which does not have it. We can study the illusory nature of our own ideas of substantial reality in three ways, first through the scriptures, second through logic, and third by the use of a metaphor.

There are many scriptural references which teach that all things in all realms of existence are merely mind. Through logic, we can begin to understand the nonexistence of phenomena by noting the power of our own minds to construct the objects which we see. All external phenomena is manifest by our own minds, in our own minds. We can compare this to being able to see some illusory thing whenever we strongly wish to do so. If we try hard enough, we can even see a rabbit with horns.

We also can use the metaphor of a dream to help us understand the illusory nature of our ideas of substantial reality. In a dream we see many things, houses, people, earth, and sky. We experience happiness, sadness, and excitement. When we awaken from the dream, it all disappears and we cannot hold on to it. In the same way, we are now in what is called the sleep of ignorance and we believe all the forms we see around us to be substantially existent phenomena. When we wake from this dream, then all the illusory appearances will vanish.

Continuing our exploration of the existence or nonexistence of objective ego, we will now examine the internal mind which is the grasper. The internal mind is refuted as being substantially existent in three ways: first by showing its momentary impermanence, second by showing that the mind as an object cannot be found, and third by showing that the mind as a subject cannot be found.

The way that the mind is refuted through momentary impermanence is by asking does the mind exist for one moment or instant or the smallest division of time? If it is asserted that the mind does exist substantially for at least the smallest division of time, then we have to analyze that smallest division to see if we can find the three times within it.

If the smallest division of time can be further divided, then that smallest instant of the mind's existence cannot be found. If it is asserted that mind exists over a period of time, that is, over a number of instants, it is refuted in the same way. If it does not exist within each of these single instants, then how can it exist over any period of it? So the mind's existence is refuted in this way.

The second way in which the mind is refuted as being a substantially existent object is by looking for it directly. In this search we employ every one of the senses to try to find its shape, its color, its size, and any possible physical attribute. We also try to find the location of it in our own body. We undertake this search with the dedication not to stop until we have directly seen the mind. But no matter how long or hard we search for any evidence of its existence, we cannot find it. This object has no color or shape to be found.

Having looked everywhere for the mind, we turn inward and look for the mind which seeks for the mind. In doing so, the mind is still not found. In this way the search for the mind is ended when we cannot find it anywhere. After this search in which the mind can never be found, the existence of the mind as a substantially existent entity can no longer be accepted.

In one of the sutras, the Buddha says to his disciple Kashyapa that the mind does not exist internally, externally, or somewhere between the two. The great teacher Tilopa also said that the mind, from the point of view of the ultimate insight into reality, cannot be expressed as existent nor can it be an object in any way to be experienced.

The third way in which the internal mind as grasper is refuted is as a substantially existent subject. If we accept the mind as subject, then it can exist only in relation to object.

As external phenomena have been shown to be nonexistent, there is no way that the internal or subjective mind can be substantially existent. Its existence as a subject depends on an object which does not exist.

Further, the inner subjective mind is refuted by showing that it cannot be subtantially existent as it has none of the attributes of existence such as size, color, shape, or form. In this way the subject mind is refuted. This completes the first argument which is the refutation of substantial existence of subjective and objective phenomena. The second argument refutes the opposite belief in the nonexistence of subjective and objective phenomena.

Now that we have shown the nonsubstantial existence of the subjective and objective phenomena, the question arises, "If they do not exist, are they nonexistent?" The answer is no, they are not nonexistent. We would think that the refutation of subjective and objective phenomena that was just presented would mean that it is possible to say that they are nonexistent, but this is not so. In order for phenomena to be nonexistent, they once would have had to have existed and then not exist. It has been proven that phenomena have no substantial existence; therefore they cannot then be nonexistent. The assertations that phenomena do exist and that they do not exist are both incorrect. The truth lies beyond the distinction or dichotomy between existence and nonexistence.

The great Mahasiddha Saraha said that if you believe that phenomena truly exist, then you are stupid like all living beings. But if you believe that nothing exists, then you are even more stupid. The explanation of the fallacy of believing in nonexistence begins with a question. If believing in the substantial existence of phenomena is the cause of the ignorance which leads to samsara, then will belief in nonexistence bring liberation? The answer is not only no, but the fallacy of holding this belief is even worse than the fallacy of believing in existence. The example given here is that if we are ill, and take medicine in an improper dosage, it may cure the illness but it also may destroy the body. Shunyata is like a medicine which cures us of our belief in existent phenomena. However, if we misunderstand it and cling to it as if it were just a negative concept, it becomes a poison which leads us to lower existence. Nagarjuna states in the *Ratnavali* that holding to the existence of phenomena leads to samsaric birth as human being or god. Holding to nonexistence destroys motivation and the belief in karma. This causes us to give up virtuous actions which will alter our karma, leading to a lower rebirth.

The refutation of the belief in a combination of existence and nonexistence comprises the fallacies of both arguments. The belief in substantial existence of phenomena is called "eternalism;" the belief in nonexistence is called "nihilism." When we mix the two, we have the short-comings of both. The specific result of nihilism is to fall into the lower realms of delusion from which one does not attain liberation.

The explanation of the path of liberation is what is called the Middle Path or Madhyamika. This is the path between the extremes of existence and nonexistence. Atisha stated that in approaching an understanding of Madhyamika, the Middle Path, we must understand the mind. The mind itself does not exist in the past because the past is finished, it does not exist in the future because the future has not arisen, and it does not exist in the present because it is impossible to find it. It has no relation or connection to shape or size or color and it is said to be like the sky, like empty space.

The explanation of nirvana, the essence of liberation, begins with Nagarjuna's teaching that the existence of nirvana as some substantial or physically existent phenomenon cannot be proved, nor can we say that it is nonexistent. If nirvana were a substantially established phenomenon, then it would be a product composed of parts and subject to dissolution and destruction. Nirvana has none of these qualities. Neither is nirvana nonexistent since we have proved that there is no nonexistence. Nirvana is beyond expression and cannot be grasped intellectually. This completes the explanation of the meaning of wisdom of the greater variety.

The *cultivation of wisdom* is compared to the process of extracting silver from silver ore. Just as we must work to separate out the valuable silver from the ore, so must we work to acknowledge the true emptiness of all things.

The practice of the cultivation of the perfection of wisdom is fourfold, consisting of preliminaries, practice, fruits, and signs of progress. The preliminaries involve setting up the proper situation of isolating the body. The practice is the stabilization of meditation, setting the mind in a state which is totally free from activity such as thinking, desiring, or conceptualizing. The mind is left to rest in its own natural condtion, its own primal state.

The fruits of cultivating wisdom are that the mind abides in the three different states of daily activity. When we go about our activities, it is with the understanding that all things are illusory and not substantially existent; when we sit down in a state of stillness, our mind is stabilized on emptiness; and when we rest or sleep, our mind does not wander from this understanding of the true nature of phenomena. The signs of progress in cultivating wisdom are that we have a great knowledge, clairvoyance, and power to perform miraculous activity with our minds unaffected; and all these achievements are undisturbed by arrogance or negative emotional patterns.

The *results of practicing wisdom* are twofold, the ultimate and the temporary. The ultimate result is the attainment of perfect peerless enlightenment. The temporary results are many, ranging from long life and freedom from illness to the acquisition and enjoyment of all the desirable things in the universe.

Questions

What are the five psychosomatic constituents?

These five constituents (skandhas) in the ordinary sense are the personality; in the purified sense they become the five Buddha families. The skandhas are form, feeling, perception, intention, and consciousness. These five constituents of existence are the raw material used by the force of our ignorance to create our samsaric existence. We compulsively grasp them through our ignorance. As we do away with ignorance in the process of liberation, we no longer compulsively take up the five psychosomatic constituents of existence and in this way the five Buddha families are achieved.

It seems to me that there are many things that arise besides the mind. It is hard for me to think that we create trees and flowers. Can you demonstrate how we do that? If everything arises in the mind and is created by the mind, that has to include trees and flowers.

The burden of proof is said to be upon the person who perceives things externally established as truly existent. The teaching here is that it is only by the force of our own ignorance that we do not perceive this manifest reality as the creation of our minds. When we do away with the klesas and destroy ignorance, all this becomes clear and there is no doubt about it. But as long as we are covered over by the darkness of ignorance and do not see reality, we think that external things are truly existent and not made by our minds.

If you ask how this can be proven to you, just think of your dreams. If you are told that the things you see are not truly existent but are a product of your own mind, you will not understand that while you are dreaming. You see flowers in your dreams, you see trees, you eat food, and when you eat it, you have sensations arising from it. It is all very real to you and in the context of the dream it never occurs to you that this is the product of your own mind. You believe everything to be truly existent and you respond in that way. But when you wake from the dream, then it is quite open and manifest that this was all the product of your own mind.

The dreams that we experience at night when we go to sleep are merely ephemeral things that come and go and are very easy to wake up from. The sleep which we are sleeping now and the dreams we are dreaming now are much more infinitely profound and hard to wake up from. They are the beginningless dreams of ignorance. That is why we call Buddhahood the "great awakening." It is the awakening from this beginningless dream of ignorance. Does that prove it to you?

Maybe I don't understand phenomena but I'm looking at this pitcher of water and I have a couple of questions about it. If I leave the room is this pitcher of water still there? Does everyone see the same pitcher of water that I see? The reason I'm asking this is because if phenomena don't have intrinsic value and are created by our minds, then does this phenomenon of the pitcher of water become a reality in my mind when I'm consciously envisioning it or looking at it with my eyes? When I leave the room or am not looking at that pitcher of water, I assume that the pitcher of water is still there; and I assume that, if someone else sees it and I'm not here, that the pitcher of water is still there unless somebody threw the pitcher of

water out of the window. Will you talk about the existence of this pitcher?

There are various aspects to your question. The "existence" of anything in the context of your own perception happens only when three things come together. These are your mind, your sense power, and the object. As long as these three things are joined together, for instance when you are sitting here and observing the water pitcher, then this object "exists" for you. When you go outside or close your eyes, you are no longer perceiving it and we can say that it no longer "exists" for you because you will have other objects that your mind is manifesting which exist for you at that time.

As to whether you see the same pitcher as someone else, the answer is that you probably are seeing a very similar one. The reason is that your karma is very similar and things exist for you through your karma. For example, if hungry ghosts were to come and look at that they would not see a container of water but a vessel of excrement or filth of some variety. If divine beings came and looked at it, they would not see water but a heavenly ambrosia. What you see is based upon your own karma. Just about all the inhabitants of this planet have similar karma and so perceive things in pretty much the same way. We can relate to each other about them. I hope that answers your question. Until we attain Buddhahood, these things are still very much hidden from us.

I can understand that the Buddha would see the pitcher differently than a human would see it. Does the pitcher dissolve in the Buddha's awakening or will it still have its own reality?

Having obtained the position of Buddhahood it is said that one can stay on the border of existence and nonexistence and either manifest things or not manifest them according to the needs of living beings. The Buddha is involved in doing whatever is beneficial for sentient beings, so if the existence of something would be beneficial, then the Buddha manifests it; if not, he does not manifest it. He has the power, the free will to either have things exist or not exist.

Does the pitcher have the free will to exist of itself or not?

An object like a pitcher of water does not have a mind so we cannot even talk about it having the free will to exist or not exist. Until we obtain the state of Buddhahood, we perceive objects as being truly existent in their own right, independent from us. With Buddhahood, we realize the truth of the matter: Objects have no such independent existence or self-existence.

After Milarepa attained enlightenment, things no longer existed for him as before. He no longer ignorantly accepted that things existed in the way that they appeared, and so without being hindered with false ideas about the existence of external phenomena, he was no longer under their power. But he also had the freedom to use them. If he wanted to walk twenty feet, he would not be hindered by the presence of a wall. If he wanted to sit where I am, but five feet up in the air, he could do that just as well. That's what it means to transcend the acceptance of external existence.

If a person passes through walls as though they do not exist, but to others they exist, it is obviously some sort of energy force. Is the person passing through the wall molecularly bonding with it, or is he dissolving molecularly and passing through? Or is he taking the middle path?

You and the wall and the act of going from here to there are all part of the illusion. When someone has gone beyond illusion and attained Buddhahood, this dualism no longer exists. In other words, his own mind, his own body, the wall, everything is of the same nature, it is all empty, empty of any substantial existence whatever. It does not truly exist. Its existence is not truly established in any way. Therefore going from here to there through the wall is not a question of separate things going from here to there. There is no dualism so there is no question of any joining of particles or destruction of particles.

The attainment of Buddhahood is a transcending of the limitations of this world totally, gaining us a state of freedom, a state of being unhindered by anything. The qualities of the Buddha are great, and those who become aware of his qualities have a great sense of faith and devotion. If Milarepa thought to himself, "I am sitting here. I will get up and walk through that wall," and really conceived of the wall as a truly existent object or himself as a truly existent object, then there would be no possibility of performing such an act. It is only because his mind was totally freed from such dichotomies by the process of becoming enlightened that he was able to do such things.

Will you say more about the qualities of our existence from the wisdom of the lesser variety?

The Hinayana practitioner meditates on four qualities to refute samsara. First, we have the thirty-six bodily impurities; second, we are unsatisfied and constantly require change, i.e., warmer, cooler, more, less, etc.; third, we are impermanent and will die; and fourth, we are egoless, that is, we don't have an ego and think that we do.

The goals of the Three Vehicles are rather different. The Hinayana goal is the egolessness of the personality which is called "arhatship." Meditating on the four qualities just listed is a vehicle for achieving that goal. The Mahayana goal is the egolessness of phenomena, which is described as tenth-level Bodhisattvahood. The Vajrayana goal is the egolessness of both personality and phenomena, and the level of achievement is beyond even tenth-level Bodhisattvahood.

I am a little confused about how the self and other are created. How do we create the self?

Well, all this around us comes from ignorance, including the self, or ego. In the first refutation, we are saying that once we believe that the ego "exists," then everything else, all phenomena, "exist"—that is, we create all this by our belief in it. Ego creates phenomena which encourage us to believe in the ego, and so on. It is like the chicken and the egg. They are a continuum, a cycle, creating each other. What we have to do to practice wisdom is to break the egg— to cut out the root of ego. The ideal of all practice is to smash the egg of ego. But it is a tough egg to crack, a tough shell. . . .

Is mind ignorant? Are our minds really full of ignorance?

The true mind is perfectly clear. Egolessness is true mind. Ignorance obscures that clarity. If you cover your eyes, your sight, what is left? Your imagination will cause you to "see," but you probably won't "see" what is really here. In just the same way ignorance clouds and distorts the vision of the true mind.

When you talked about subatomic particles, you said that if we insist that these particles are indivisible, then we can easily see that these particles are not identical with all things. Don't we know from physics that there are particles forming the basis of all things?

What we know about subatomic particles is that they are the basis of part of the whole, but are not identical to all of the whole. For instance, let us say you have a whole teapot and then it breaks. No one of those pieces is the teapot. It may be a part of the side or bottom or lid or spout, but it is only a part of the whole. In that way, no piece or particle is identical to the whole of existence.

What do Bodhisattvas see? If they know that everything is empty, do they even see our world?

They see the world they are in and deeply know that it is not real. They are in a relative world so they see both the relative and absolute worlds. Because they are here to help us in the phenomenal world, they will see it and work with it.

When you talk about believing in nonexistence, it sounds like Existentialism. If nothing is real, why is it so bad to believe in that?

If we hold to nonexistence, it is not out of knowing emptiness but just from denying existence. What we need to avoid is grasping desperately to either existence or nonexistence. The grasping comes from our ignorance, not our wisdom.

How do we practice Madhyamika, the Middle Path?

If you practice wisdom and skillful means, it will take you to shamatha (object meditation). This will naturally lead you to vipasyana (emptiness meditation) which will take you to the answer to your question!

Section III:
Approach to Tantra

Chapter One
Basic Approach to the
Tantric Path

The tantric path to enlightenment is a quick path and very effective, but it all depends on us. This is not a path that will carry us passively to Buddhahood. We must walk the entire distance ourselves, and to do so we must first make preparations for the journey.

The first qualification is a deep understanding of the Four Foundations (Section I, Chapter 1) which motivates us to take this journey. We have the rare opportunity of the precious human existence which is the result of past virtuous deeds. The human realm is the only one from which we can reach enlightenment, so this life is not one to waste.

Impermanence is a fact of our existence. We will soon die, though we don't know when it will happen. That uncertainty motivates us to cultivate virtuous habits by performing beneficial deeds in the short time available to us.

Our human existence shows us some of the suffering of the phenomenal world. The sufferings of suffering and change are constant reminders of the need to escape from samsara, the cycle of rebirth.

The raw material of samsaric existence is karma. Our actions in each life bear fruit in future ones and we do not have the freedom to escape. We are controlled by the winds of our karma like a feather on the wind and only beneficial actions can keep us on the path to permanent happiness.

The second qualification for the tantric path is a relationship with a spiritual friend (Section I, Chapter 3) who gives guidance and blessings for the journey. We cannot see the many enlightened teachers around us, so we rely on the ordinary spiritual friend who is here with us in samsara. This person is our guide on the tantric path and therefore the most important person in the world to us. It is our responsibility as students to cultivate this relationship by showing respect, making offerings, and, most of all, taking in the teachings and doing the practice.

The third qualification is our compassion for sentient beings (Section II) which magnifies the benefits of our actions. The enlightened attitude arises from compassion for the suffering of others; compassion arises directly from the loving kindness we have experienced in our lives. This loving kindness is compared to a mother's love, and since all beings have been our mothers, our gratitude toward them becomes the basis for selflessly dedicating all our efforts toward enlightenment.

In summary, the Four Foundations motivate us, the teacher gives us guidance and blessings, and compassion magnifies our actions. These three fundamentals are the basis for the tantric path which the succeeding chapters will discuss.

Chapter Two
Methods of Visualization
and Meditation

The tantric practice of visualization always begins with having the proper attitude. We take time to generate Bodhi Mind, the awareness that we seek liberation and do this practice to benefit all living beings. This pure motivation prevents the practice from building our egos. Whatever deity we visualize, it is important to concentrate one-pointedly so that both the deity and its attributes are very clear. The deity must also be seen as nonsubstantial and transparent like a rainbow, but unlike a rainbow, the deity is a form of emptiness and great purity. This process of visualizing the deity is known as the development stage. When we have completed the visualization, the deity melts into light and disappears into emptiness. This dissolving stage completes the visualization. This is followed by emptiness meditation, beyond intellect and beyond conceptualization.

However, most of us who are just beginning meditation practice have difficulty generating clear visualizations and dissolving them into emptiness. To develop concentration, we can practice various meditational techniques. A very simple way to begin is to focus on our breath. We sit still and upright and just breathe in and out; there is no special way to breathe. The average healthy person will breathe about 500 times each hour. We simply need to sit down in a quiet place and focus our attention on our breathing. We watch the breath come into the body, pause within the body, and leave the body. Occupying our minds with this inhalation and exhalation leaves no room for the emotions to arise. The six poisonous emotions of ignorance, desire, anger, jealousy, greed, and pride, which cause us to be born in the six realms, are completely controlled when we watch our breath in this manner. Concentrating on our breath also reduces our habitual tendency to produce these negative emotions. So, in a way, the mind is protected by this method of meditation. Our ability to focus the mind on the breath is not, in itself, the realization of emptiness, but it is an important step toward that goal.

After developing the ability to watch the breath in this way, we can advance our practice by counting each breath. Mistakes in counting will quickly tell us when our mind is wandering, and our concentration will become more refined. As the mind becomes calm with the repeated practice of this meditational technique, we may develop temporary or immature omniscience. Of course, if we stop meditating, this omniscience is exhausted and we return to our original agitated state.

Focusing on the breath develops a very strong mind which can maintain its stability and attention to the breath during any external activity of the body. Although this is basically a Hinayana technique, it is still a fundamental for Mahayana and Vajrayana practitioners, for if we do not know the Hinayana we cannot know the Mahayana or Vajrayana.

This meditation sequence is similar to the process of going to school. As children, we learn to read and write and we learn all the special skills of being in a group. Day by day we progress until finally we go to high school and perhaps even to college. What happens if we skip high school and go straight to college? We won't understand the lectures or homework unless we are a genius. Likewise, if we skip the meditational techniques of the Hinayana and Mahayana in our haste to get to the Vajrayana, we will not have the skills to understand the new techniques unless we have really exceptional karma. Even those with extraordinary karma and very high reincarnated beings still go through the whole meditational process, though they will do it more quickly than most of us.

A Mahayana practitioner may develop concentration by focusing on an object, for example a small visualized sphere or dot at the level of the nose and ten fingers' distance in front of the face. Concentrating one-pointedly on this, we absorb the mind fully in this object. Once we develop the concentration on this single point, we can add four spheres at a further distance—one in front, one behind, and one each to the left and right. All have the same shape, size, and color. We then focus the mind on these five points at the same time. Once we are able to focus on these five and develop perfect concentration on them, we can then visualize the spheres in the four directions merging into the one in front of us. Then the one in front is seen to grow smaller and smaller until it disappears completely, merging into space. After training in this technique and developing some proficiency in this, we may be ready to visualize the deities of the Vajrayana.

It is important to distinguish here the techniques of the Hinayana and Mahayana. It is said that there are three stages to any Mahayana practice. The first stage is generating a pure motivation to benefit sentient beings; at the beginning of any meditation, we should think of liberating all beings from samsaric suffering through this practice. The second stage is during the actual practice. We should concentrate deeply on whatever object we are using and the mind should be fully absorbed in that concentration. The third stage is prior to ending the meditation. We should dedicate any virtues gained from this practice to all sentient beings so that all their suffering may cease. These three stages, the generation of an enlightened attitude, concentration, and dedication of merit, distinguish the Mahayana techniques from those of the Hinayana.

It can be very helpful to change methods from time to time to prevent our minds from becoming bored. When we are bored, we get sleepy; our concentration falters and all our efforts fail. By changing techniques, we are actually playing a game with the mind; we are practicing different means to accomplish the same end. The mind is like a cat. If a cat is in a cage, it will always want to get out, and it will claw and scream to get our attention. When we open the door, the cat leaves the cage but it has no particular place to go. The mind, like the cat, quickly becomes bored with its present activity. Only disciplined concentration will take us beyond boredom.

After developing concentration through the Hinayana methods of watching and counting the breaths, and the Mahayana method of concentrating on an object, we may be ready to begin a Vajrayana technique. One tantric method is known as the Vajra Recitations and involves silently reciting the syllable OM as we breath in, AH as we pause, and HUNG as we breathe out. The syllable OM is the embodiment of the Buddha's body, AH is the embodiment of the Buddha's speech, and HUNG, the embodiment of the Buddha's mind. These three syllables express the Buddha's wisdom with its vajra-like indestructibility. Our ordinary body, speech, and mind are plagued by the negative emotions. Silent recitation of the vajra syllables OM, AH, HUNG purifies us due to the pure nature of the Buddha's body, speech, and mind which is free from karma and the conflicting emotions. This method is more powerful than the pacification of the negative emotions that is accomplished by the previous techniques. Vajra Recitation not only reduces our habitual tendency toward the afflicted emotions, but it also purifies the root poisons of anger, desire, and ignorance.

Another Vajrayana method to develop emptiness or Mahamudra is visualization of deities. In this form of visualization, it is important to remember that the deities are not substantial in any way. We view the deities as emptiness. In the beginning, it is difficult to visualize the deities in a clear and detailed manner. However, with repeated practice and effort, our mind stabilizes and the image of the deities becomes vivid.

The deities manifest in many forms, some with multiple arms, faces, and colors. Each detail might represent the wisdom of the Buddhas, all-pervasive compassion, loving kindness, joyfulness and equanimity, or other enlightened activity. The way we approach a complete and clear visualization is to understand what all these details are and what they represent. However, even in all their detail, the deities must remain nonsubstantial with bodies like rainbows. No realization can be attained from envisioning the deities as if they were solid like statues. After intellectually understanding the forms and details of the deities, we can develop faith and devotion in their enlightened attributes. This faith and devotion will help to clarify our visualization.

During the visualization of the tantric divinities, we practice the experience of the three supramundane activities. These three activities are called the *Three Kayas* or *Three Bodies,* and they each have three facets or aspects. These are the *Basis Three Kayas,* the *Path Three Kayas,* and the *Result Three Kayas.* Constituting the *Basis Three Kayas* are our own speech, mind, and body on the mundane level. The *Path Three Kayas* are the engagement of the body, speech, and mind in pure and perfect conduct or performance during the practice of the Deities' Yogas. The **Result Three Kayas** are realizing that the true nature of the mind is emptiness which is very clear and luminous; as there is no attachment to the emptiness and clarity, it is completely unimpeded.

As for the **Basis Three Kayas,** these are hidden in our mundane activities; the pure Three Kayas are within our body, speech, and mind, obscured by our conflicting emotions which are caused by our ego clinging. This creates impure activity and the result of this is painful both physically and mentally. The mind has no energy, the speech has no power, and the body has no strength. This leads us through the cycle of existence.

Concerning the **Path Three Kayas,** first there is the Dharmakaya, or Truth Body; in any of the Tantric visualizations, before we visualize, we must view complete emptiness of self and all phenomena. This is the experience of the Truth Body of the Path (Dharmakaya). Out of the emptiness appears a lotus and moon seat and the seed syllable of the deity, and from that the complete form of the deity arises with all its perfect ornaments and attributes. This we call the Enjoyment Body of the Path (Sambhogakaya). After having visualized the deity perfectly and precisely, then we radiate light to transform all defilement and impurity; thus the external world becomes the pure land and mandala of the divinity, while internally all living beings become the deity's entourage. This is the Emanation Body of the Path (Nirmanakaya).

These **Path Three Kayas** are very important. If we practice in this way, we can transform the mundane world to the supramundane blissful realm or mandala. These **Path Three Kayas** also correspond to the experiences we have in life, death, and the intermediate state or bardo. The dissolving into emptiness of the Truth Body of the Path is like the death experience. The practice of the Enjoyment Body of the Path—visualizing the lotus-moon seat, and the deity arising from the appropriate seed letters—corresponds to the bardo experience, the attraction toward new parents, and the conception of a new body which is then born in the world. The activities of this new body correspond to the Emanation Body of the Path or Nirmanakaya. For a more detailed explanation of this, one can read my book, *Bardo Teachings, The Way of Death and Rebirth* (Revised Edition, KDK Publications, 1982).

It is also important to note that during these visualizations we must follow the different, specific tantric sadhanas. To do this we need the instruction of a qualified lama who can give the explanation of the more detailed description and the precise practice involved. In general, all are the same: While visualizing, we must have great compassion toward all sentient beings and great devotion to the deities, which are inseparable from the root guru, and view the deities as insubstantial yet clear in their appearance and inseparable from emptiness.

The **Basis Three Kayas** are the seed from which the **Path Three Kayas** grow. The fruit produced by this is the **Result Three Kayas.** The first of these is the **Resulting Truth Body,** which is completely empty and beyond all conceptualization, yet expresses all enlightened qualities. The **Resulting Enjoyment Body** is the expression of emptiness as complete clarity and luminosity. It is not at all numb, trance-like, or dark nothingness but is the manifestation of great mercy and objectless compassion. The **Resulting Emanation Body** is the unobstructed quality of this clarity and luminosity, appearing in the form most appropriate to whomever requires disciplining or benefiting.

When we are doing any of these forms of meditation, it is important to be disciplined. A short meditation done daily is superior to irregular meditations in terms of building our ability to concentrate. If we set a time period of ten minutes a day, we should meditate for that amount of time rather than skipping it or sitting for two hours instead. We must avoid being too attached or repelled by meditation; if we do much more or less than our daily stint, we increase the risk of stopping altogether.

We have to be very skillful with our minds. We need discipline to limit the mind's likes and dislikes in meditation as in other areas of life. When we get caught up in the endless chatter about what kind or how much meditation to do, it is as if there is a devil inside of us. Of course we all have devils within that come from our selfish egos. Sometimes we believe there are devils outside of us, too, which are going to harm us, but they are a reflection of our inner doubts and terror. When I was a boy, my family owned a herd of cattle and at night the calves were protected from wild animals by forms dressed to look like people. I came to the herder's camp one night and saw a person beckoning to me. When I came close, the person tried to catch me. Of course I screamed and everyone came to see what was wrong but they couldn't find any kidnappers. In the morning I saw that my monster was a bamboo basket with clothes and a big stick put onto it. I had created the devil's actions and menace myself.

All of us have evils, fears, doubts, and hatreds within us. If we let our ego have its way, we will one day decide, "I must be someone special because I meditated for two hours," and another day we will say, "I'm not going to meditate; I'm just not in the mood." The ego is fickle and will resist the discipline of meditating every day for the same amount of time, but this discipline is the only thing which can break the lazy and frivolous habits of samsara.

Whatever meditation technique we are practicing, it is important that our minds not dwell on the past, present, or future. When we meditate, we sometimes find ourselves recalling the past. We may be thinking of what we have or have not done in some particular moment. This recollection of past events is a definite obstruction to our concentration or emptiness meditation. Likewise projecting our thoughts into the future also creates obstacles to our meditations. If we begin to think about what we may do in the next hour or the next day, we are creating further delusions for ourselves.

If we avoid the past and do not create the future, we might think we have found the middle ground and can now proceed in our meditations without further distractions, but this is not necessarily true. It is all too easy to attach ourselves to the present and begin to analyze or judge it. We might think, "Oh, I'm not meditating perfectly. I should be more relaxed or sitting in a better posture;" or we might say to ourselves, "Yes, this is a good meditation. Now I've really achieved emptiness. This is great." All thoughts of the past, present, or future should be avoided so that the mind can rest naturally.

In general, there are two types of meditation which I have been describing. First, I described shamatha (Tib: sheenay) which means "calming." Concentrating on the breath, the OM-AH-HUNG meditation, and the sphere visualization are all examples of shamatha meditation. There are two levels of shamatha. Ordinary shamatha requires effort and determination to effectively calm the mind. Extraordinary shamatha is the more mature level, when calm abiding arises naturally and without effort. In the Diamond Vehicle, in order for the mind to achieve a more perfect stability, there is a special method to practice this mature, undistracted shamatha. This is the level of the Deity's Yoga called the Development Stage (Tib: Kye Rim).

The second type of meditation I've been describing is called vipasyana (Tib: lhatong), which means "insight." Attempting to keep our minds relaxed and free of attachment to the past, present, or future is a vipasyana meditation. The Mahasiddha Saraha said that we search and search for the mind and cannot find anything. Not finding anything is the goal, the "insight." Again, as with shamatha meditation, there are two levels of vipasyana. Ordinary vipasyana requires our full attention, effort, and diligence to improve our concentration and gain insight. When our meditation practice has matured, extraordinary vipasyana requires no effort but arises spontaneously and leads to enlightenment. In the Diamond Vehicle the special practice of this mature, extraordinary vipasyana is the level of Deity Yoga called the Completion or Accomplishment Stage (Tib: Dzog Rim).

The union of shamatha and vipasyana meditaiton is called Nyam-shak, which means "equalizing." When we try to do emptiness meditation, we must deal with the five skandhas, each of which has characteristics. The skandha of form is characterized by breakability and destructibility, the skandha of feeling by experience or desire, the skandha of perception by following the object, the skandha of intention by performing actions, and the skandha of consciousness by creation of objects. These five worldly skandhas are the causes of suffering and rebirth. Nyam-shak meditation unites the calming of our shamatha meditations and the insight of our vipasyana meditations to produce four characteristics of our minds: luminosity, clarity, radiance, and absence of conceptualization. The mind learns to be unattached to form itself, to experience (the skandha of feeling), to discrimination and separation (the skandha of perception), to motivation (the skandha of intention), and to clinging to phenomena (the skandha of consciousness).

The exchange of the five skandhas for the four characteristics of Nyam-shak meditation is a sophisticated and difficult technique. We would do well to remember that even the Buddha started as a beginner, an ordinary person who was willing to work for something beyond what was obviously available in this world. We, too, have Buddha nature, the potential for awakening; we also possess the precious human existence, the knowledge of right and wrong, and the ability to understand new ideas. So we should try to practice these forms of meditation, for it is our effort alone which will lead us to enlightenment.

Commentary on this subject of shamatha and vipasyana, Nyam-shak, development stage, and completion stage can be extended into volumes or condensed into a very few lines. The explanation depends on the teacher and the needs of the students. I have here given a very brief introduction to these meditations and how they are connected on the path which the Buddha taught. It is important to remember that while these techniques may be presented in many different ways, they are all the teachings of the Buddha. We can have confidence in them and should seek a qualified teacher to guide us and monitor our progress in them.

There are many other forms of meditation. But if these few are not practiced, what value would more methods be? If I pour water into a glass and keep pouring more and more, the glass will overflow; if I describe more and more methods of meditation, you will overflow also. At some point, it is time to stop talking and start acting.

Questions

Many spiritual paths encourage some form of meditation, but visualization seems to be unique to the Vajrayana. What is the purpose of visualization?

Meditation and visualization both teach concentration. When you concentrate on your breath, you increase your ability to focus, but this method can only bring "ordinary" results since you are focusing on an ordinary object—your breath. When you concentrate on visualizing a deity, you also increase your ability to focus, but this method can bring "extraordinary" results because you are focusing on an extraordinary object—a deity. By viewing the deity as emptiness, your mind is purified; by reciting mantra, your speech is purified; by visualizing the deity, your body is purified.

When you do a deity visualization, you can keep the mind fully occupied by making each detail—posture, ornaments, garments, ritual objects, etc.—clear in your mind's eye. This keeps your mind fully occupied, rather than bored, and allows your mind to rest in the qualities of enlightenment.

There are several styles of visualization. Briefly, in Upa Tantra visualization, you would see yourself as a servant before a powerful ruler. You would want to make no mistakes in their presence, so you would avoid the conflicting emotions. Thus this method is a way of pacifying the poisons.

Kriya Tantra visualization places the deity in the position of a parent. You would strive to please them and this would become the motivation for virtuous actions and diligent practice.

Yoga Tantra visualization views the deity and the meditator as identical. The deity is emptiness with appearance and you/the deity become the vehicle to achieving emptiness with clarity. The final stage of this tantra, Maha Yoga, is emptiness with awareness.

It is very easy for us to visualize some things such as our friends and our parents. I still find it difficult, though, to visualize the deities and their mandalas. What can I do to improve?

The traditional way to improve your visualization is to learn to paint the deity and mandalas complete in every detail. You could also make a sincere offering to an artist to render a painting. If the representation were done, your visualization would improve due to the sincerity of your offering.

Generally, if your visualizations are unclear, then you are not doing enough virtuous actions. Practice the Six Perfections, the Vajrasattva mantra, Ngöndro, Nyung Nes, and making offerings. When you do your practice devotedly, your visualizations will improve naturally.

What can we do when we feel deep physical or emotional pain during meditation? Or when there's a loud noise that interrupts us?

When you have physical pain during meditation, you can transform it by thinking of the great pains of all sentient beings. Dissolve their pain into yours and yours into emptiness. When you feel emotional or mental pain, remember those pains throughout the six realms and especially in the human realm. Collect all that pain into yours and purify it for all by letting it dissolve into emptiness. To remember and take on the pain of others is the Mahayana way.

If something interrupts you at meditation, try to be patient and dedicate that effort toward your development of limitless patience. Remember to be thankful for the interruptions, for without them, you could not develop patience as an antidote to anger.

Chapter Three
Relative and Absolute
Points of View

This chapter concerns the two truths, relative and absolute. There are many levels of relative and absolute truth, especially when we look at them from the worldly perspective. The experience of relative reality can be compared to studying and learning in school, and the absolute reality can be compared to the attainment of knowledge which results. After finishing school, we go to work, and this is a relative experience; achieving the goals we work for is an absolute experience. Relative is what we work toward; absolute is what we achieve.

From the Buddhist perspective, learning the techniques of meditation is an "inner" relative experience; that is, it is working toward an inner goal rather than a worldly one. When we begin to use those techniques in meditation, it is an absolute experience, although an immature one.

The pure nature of the mind is the essential absolute. It is made relative by the five poisons. Our unpurified minds project illusion which we see as all the phenomena of the material world. We think these phenomena are "real" and absolute, but since they are the products of our poisoned minds, they are only illusionary and relative.

We can see how easily we can be fooled by illusion masquerading as reality if we think of a magic show. Let us say that I am a magician. I make things appear before you, a beautiful car, a horse, and a terrifying monster. I know that all of these things are not real, that all of it is a joke. However from your point of view, the magic is not a joke; you believe what you see to be real. You are attracted to the beautiful things and repelled by the terrifying things. The magician in this example is the absolute and what you see is the relative. Because you do not know that the relative comes from the absolute, you are amazed.

All of the phenomenal world is created in the same way. It is created from the pure mind itself, influenced by the poisons. From the Buddha's enlightened point of view, the relative is nothingness and the absolute is the only reality. However, from our point of view, the relative is significant because it is why we exist, so it is important that we do not deny the relative by thinking, "This is just an illusion." If we were to follow that thought to its logical conclusion, we might think we could stop eating or drinking and remain unaffected, but we would soon die. For our ego, the relative material world is our reality and we must not deny it.

Ironically, another pitfall for us is denying the absolute and thinking that the relative is the only reality. When faced with the idea that the absolute is empty, we may find it very strange and we may deny this truth from our fear. We might say to ourselves, "How can this be empty? I am here, you are here. There's a whole world around us." We are strongly attached to the relative and our fear of the absolute creates more obstacles to our comprehension that absolute emptiness is the nature of the mind. If we want anything beyond the temporary pleasures of this life, however, we must set aside our fear of the empty unknown and stop denying the absolute.

Consequently, in our efforts to achieve enlightenment, we must concentrate on both the relative and the absolute. We must care for the relative and learn skillful means in this phenomenal world rather than thinking our spiritual practice will be separate from it. The Vajrayana path is a way to keep ourselves from avoiding the relative or denying the absolute; it utilizes the relative to achieve the absolute.

The Vajrayana tradition utilizes many different techniques in its quest for emptiness. The Vajrayana teacher may instruct us to try an emptiness meditation. At another time, the instructions might be to do prostrations, recite mantras, do visualizations, or make offerings. These may seem to be contradictory instructions. At one point there is nothing to meditate on or to do, while at another point there are many things to do. However, the prostrations, mantras, visualizations, and offerings are a relative means to an absolute end. They are also a kind of immature absolute because they are relative actions being used as an antidote to relative illusions. They will lead us to a mature understanding of the absolute. The Buddha, in his wisdom and compassion, gave these techniques to destroy the relative. He also said that this tantric path is a very difficult one for ordinary beings to understand and follow. Because it is such an arduous path, we must rely on our teacher, for it would be all too easy for us to use the relative to create the relative rather than destroy it. Our teacher can help us to know the difference.

An analogy may help us when we think about the contradictions inherent in the tantric path. When we have a fire, wood is burned. The fire is the relative means to destroy the relative fuel. When there is no wood left to burn, there is no more fire; the completed process creates emptiness.

Where does relative reality come from? The phenomenal world we know arises from three intersecting components: consciousness, senses, and objects. Tantric commentaries describe eight human consciousnesses: eye consciousness,

nose consciousness, tongue consciousness, ear conscious-
ness, physical consciousness, mental consciousness, emotional consciousness, and primordial consciousness. This is
not to say that our organs—eyes, ears, nose, etc.—have their
own consciousnesses. For example, if you took the eye out
of its socket, it would no longer see anything. Rather, the
functioning perceptions of these organs connect with the activity of the mind to produce the intentional awareness (or
consciousness) specific to each of these organs. The eye, for
example, apprehends a color and form; then in conjunction
with the conscious mind it perceives an object having that
color and form. The ear apprehends sound waves; in conjunction with conscious mind, it distinguishes the nature of
the sound, a knock on the door or a musical note. In each
case the sense organ, the sensation, and the consciousness
are interdependent.

These consciousnesses are the "projectors" of the
relative; when they combine with the five senses (sight,
smell, taste, hearing, and touch) and an object, we have
what is called a "gathering." In this gathering, there are
three possible results: attraction (desire), aversion (anger), or
neutrality (ignorance). Desire, anger, and ignorance are the
three Root Poisons, and it is these poisons which lead us to
action, to karma.

We recognize that it is our minds that perform the actions
but when we look at the mind, it is empty and nowhere to
be found. If the mind is empty, how can there be karma? It
is difficult for us to believe in it if we cannot see it; if we
hear that karma will come to us in the future, it is difficult to
believe that too.

An example may aid us in comprehending the existence
of karma. When we go to school, we learn to read and write
and we may learn many other facts and skills if we choose
to do so. For instance, you may learn to be a doctor. If you
are walking down the street, no one can tell that you are a

doctor but if there is an accident, you can use your skills to help people. Your knowledge is invisible until it is needed. It is just the same with karma. We have acted in many good and bad ways in our many lifetimes and our primordial consciousness holds all that accumulated karma. It is invisible until the karma ripens and the good or bad results surface.

The primordial consciousness also stores our habitual tendencies. These are the ways in which we are likely to act, based on our experience (karma) in many lifetimes. We have the ability and will to act in certain virtuous and non-virtuous ways; when we act, we create the karma. In the previous example of studying to be a doctor, your training would have given you the habitual tendency to heal; when you actually aided someone, you would be creating karma out of that habitual tendency. Obviously, virtuous actions build the capacity for virtuous habitual tendencies and non-virtuous actions increase the potential for nonvirtuous habitual tendencies.

When we are concentrating on relative reality, that is, our samsaric existence, then karma and habitual tendencies seem to be paramount. We may resolve to increase our virtuous actions in order to increase our happiness in this and other lifetimes. However from the absolute perspective, even the happiest conditions are only temporary if we remain trapped in the karmic cycle of existence—the necessity to be endlessly reborn in order to live out the results of our actions. The only thing that can interrupt this cycle of rebirth is Buddhahood, the awakening to the ultimately empty, absolute nature of the mind. In our quest for this goal, our resolve to do virtuous actions may be seen in a new light. Virtuous activity leads to the accumulation of merit and eventually to the wisdom of enlightenment. Thus we are once again using activities in the relative reality to achieve the absolute goal.

The Three Vehicles were given by the Buddha as paths

toward purifying karma. Each vehicle takes practitioners to
different goals on the road to enlightenment and each ap-
peals to different people according to their karma. The common feature of all three vehicles is the interest in subduing
the conflicting emotions.

The Hinayana Vehicle is a practice based on the sutras,
that is, on the dialogues between Shakyamuni Buddha and
his students. The Hinayana methods of subduing the conflicting emotions concentrate on avoiding those emotions.
For example, when the emotion of desire arises, we would
contemplate the ugliness inherent in all things. If we feel
desire toward a person, we would think of all the blood and
pus and flesh that they are made of, and also would remind
ourselves of their inevitable aging and dying processes.
These contemplations would quickly turn us from the object of our desire and thus we would avoid the karma of acting on our afflicted emotions.

The Mahayana Vehicle is also based on the sutras. The
Mahayana methods of subduing emotions concentrate on
viewing all things as illusion or mirage. For example, if we
feel the desire to have a beautiful flower, we would search
that flower to find the essence of its beauty. Viewed ana-
tomically, the roots, stem, leaves, and petals do not hold any
attraction for us; we are forced to see that the beauty we
desire is not real, but merely springs from our minds. Of
course this method is equally useful when we contemplate
those things for which we feel aversion.

The Vajrayana Vehicle is based on the tantras which are
some of the esoteric teachings of the Buddha. It is described
as the quick path because, if we have access to the favorable
conditions called "ordinary siddhi," which include food,
clothing, devotion, prosperity, a teacher, good health, and
the time to practice, and if we make use of them, we can
achieve "supreme siddhi" which is enlightenment. These
favorable conditions can be more than just sources of our

temporary happiness; they can become relative tools for us to utilize in achieving the absolute.

In the tantric techniques, we neither avoid emotions nor view them as illusion. We learn, instead, to transform them. If, for example, we felt desire, we would visualize the Buddha Amitabha and this would close the door to the craving of desire. The emotion does not disappear but is exchanged with the deity as we proceed through the development stage —forming an accurate image and then visualizing ourselves as the diety—to the accomplishment stage—dissolving the visualization into emptiness.

Each conflicting emotion can be transformed by visualizing and merging with a Wisdom Buddha: Amitabha for desire, Vajrasattva for anger, Akshobya for ignorance, Amoghasiddhi for jealousy, and Ratnasambhava for pride. We can also expand this method of transformation by taking on the desire of all living beings and generating the proper attitude that all this desire be transformed by our visualization.

The most supreme tantric technique is called "nondual" tantra. It is an identification on the deepest levels that the nature of our conflicting emotions is inseparable from emptiness and bliss. Our emotions become fuel arising from the relative reality that will be burned up by our practice, leaving in their place the limitless space and clarity of the luminous absolute, the pure mind. If we are wise enough and practiced enough to utilize this technique, then we will be beyond the need to avoid emotions, see them as illusionary, or exchange them. We will be resting in Dharmakaya, with no need to "do" anything.

A story may illuminate the validity of this technique. A lady patron and student of the sage Milarepa was disturbed by her thoughts while in meditation. Milarepa sent her away to contemplate the sky. She returned and told him that the sky was clear and limitless but sometimes obscured by clouds. "Why make the sky and clouds separate things?" Milarepa asked. "The clouds come from the sky and do not change the sky in any way. They just appear to be different." The student then realized that the sky was like the mind, clear and limitless. The clouds were like thoughts, which appeared to obscure the mind but actually came from it and were not separate from it at all.

This discussion of the relative and absolute points of view has focused mainly on the relative. It is usual in our world to think of the relative as the entire reality. However, if we can embrace the idea of an absolute perspective, a fundamental wisdom perspective, then we will not only view our phenomenal world in a different way, but we can make use of it in our quest for enlightenment.

Questions

Lama, sometimes I am lazy about doing my practice. What will help me?

Meditating on impermanence can help you when you feel lazy. When you realize that you aren't going to keep your precious human existence forever, it can make you diligent in your efforts to reach enlightenment. Also, laziness can arise when you don't understand things, so doing the Manjushri puja can help because it increases your wisdom and understanding.

How does our devotion relate to the relative and absolute points of view?

When we intellectually grasp the idea of absolute reality and believe that we can attain it, the desire to do so naturally arises. We naturally become devoted to caring for the relative in skillful ways, which will take us to the absolute.

Our devotion to the goal, the path, and the guru leads us to do virtuous actions and avoid nonvirtuous ones, to generate compassion and accumulate merit.

Sometimes if I am talking with someone and we disagree, I can feel that if we keep on talking, there will be a big argument. So I stop talking because I don't want to do nonvirtuous, angry acts. But it makes people mad if I stop talking, so we're creating bad karma anyway! What should I do?

You can try to be compassionate. You could tell them what you're doing, like, "Let's not talk about this anymore. I don't want to argue with you." You could ask them what they want from you or you could say that you are trying to understand their opinion although you may not agree with it. It is good to try all these things and still you must be strong because even when you are compassionate, some people will get very angry at that.

When did the Buddha teach the tantra?

In his lifetime Shakyamuni Buddha manifested in other forms such as Vajradhara and gave the tantric teachings to Vajrapani and King Indrabodhi, among others.

You said to visualize Vajrasattva if we are angry. I don't know much about the Buddha. What should I do?

There are drawings of the five Wisdom Buddhas in my book *Bardo Teachings,* so you could use that to help you. Also, if you have other tantric initiations, you could visualize those deities—Chenrezig, Tara, Kalachakra—as the focus for transforming your conflicting emotions.

Do we use eye consciousness to visualize? If we were blind, would we use other organs of the body to see with, since we would still have eye consciousness?

When you visualize, it is not necessary, or perhaps even desirable, to use the eyes to visualize. It is the mind that visualizes. Perhaps at the beginning it is helpful to look at a picture or statue representing the deity or visualization, but later it is important to be able to generate this visualization with the mind.

A blind person should be able to visualize. For someone who has been blind from birth, it will be very hard to get an idea of what visualization is, but such a person would eventually visualize through hearing a description of the visualization or through their sense of touch.

Chapter Four
Six Gatherings on the Path
to Liberation

Here is a method to employ our daily mundane activity as an exercise to transform everything into the path of the supramundane. We have six sense organs which are influenced by the conflicting emotions. If we do not recognize the source of our consciousness, then they lead us to confusion and suffering in the cycle of existence. This chapter will describe how to use the daily activity of the sense organs to carry us on the Path of Liberation.

The senses arise from the consciousness and with these senses we perceive objects, which also arise from the consciousness. A "gathering" is the conjunction of object, sense, and consciousness. Feelings such as ignorance, desire, anger, pride, and jealousy arise when we perceive objects, and when we act on these feelings, we create karma.

For example, for a man to fall in love with a woman, several things must be present. First, there must be the subject, in this case the man who is perceiving, and the object, in this case the woman. Second, the subject must have both sense and consciousness. If he lacked eyes, he could not see the object; if he lacked consciousness, he could not receive the impression of his senses.

From the conjunction of the senses, the consciousness, and the object comes a "gathering." Quite naturally from the gathering the conflicting emotions arise. The man desires the woman. If she does not return this feeling, anger arises, and if she actually loves another, jealousy arises. If he thinks he must win her from another and control her, pride arises. If she loves him but he fears her spending time with other people, greed arises.

A similar situation occurs if this man sees an enemy. When he first sees this enemy, hatred or anger arises. From this hatred comes the thought that he must defeat his enemy, which is a feeling of pride. All the conflicting emotions will arise in this example of aversion just as they arose in the previous example of attraction. The presence of the conflicting emotions leads us to develop habits of thought, generating the tendency to act, which leads to karmic results. These habitual tendencies accumulate and reinforce themselves day after day, year after year, and lifetime after lifetime.

The senses, through which we experience so much of the phenomenal world, are sight, smell, taste, hearing, and touch. In addition, the consciousness itself is numbered as the sixth sense, since it is the basis for all sense experience. It is always the consciousness which knows. This is like putting a monkey in a house with five windows. As the monkey rushes around from window to window, it seems that there are many monkeys, but really there is just one busy monkey. In the same way, we have senses which reflect one "busy" consciousness.

The conjunction of the six senses with objects and consciousness forms six gatherings, which all humans experience constantly. Samsara arises from the six gatherings.

It is possible to employ these six gatherings on the path to liberation. The first step is to recognize the occurrence of a gathering. For instance, when we see something beautiful and our desire arises, we would not repress our desire but would examine it to discover if it had any substance. We would ask ourselves, "What is this desire? What is its shape, color, location, etc.?" Not finding any of these, we realize that this emotion is without substance and we need not follow it; this desire has no reality, the feeling dissolves into emptiness, and we can relax our minds in meditation. When we analyze the situation in this way, we banish our desire.

Since there is no desire, none of the other emotions arise, and the object which was desired dissolves into consciousness. Subject, object, and sense are interdependent. If the object is found to be insubstantial and unreal, the sense and subject must also be insubstantial and unreal. All three then dissolve into consciousness, and finally the consciousness itself dissolves into Dharmakaya. Since the five poisons no longer exist, ignorance, which is their foundation, is exhausted, and this is the liberation.

Whenever any of the Six Gatherings arise from seeing, hearing, tasting, etc., we should not repress them but should use them in our meditation in the same way as described for desire. If we can practice this, then the more that poisons such as desire arise, the greater the benefit will be. When the poisons arise, we can have a greater understanding of the foundation of our mind. Freedom comes from the practice of using the six gatherings to liberate ourselves from the karma of the poisons.

Chapter Five
Viewing Emptiness

Emptiness cannot easily be expressed. It has no form, no color, no shape, no subject, or object. Yet the realization of emptiness is wisdom itself, the most important result of all our practice. Naturally we look for it everywhere. When we meditate, we are searching; we have this great expectation that we are going to find something. The Mahasiddha Saraha said that he himself looked for a long time to find something as a result of his meditation. He could not find anything and finally realized that there was nothing to be found. This realization of emptiness was what he had sought all along. When we find complete emptiness, we will have found what we are looking for.

To realize this perfect emptiness called Mahamudra, we must first subdue our minds. The mind is naturally empty, so there is really nothing there to subdue. "Subduing the mind" actually means subduing the conflicting emotions. These conflicting emotions cannot be located as they have no color, shape, or size. However, we can clearly feel their painful results. The Buddha compared subduing the mind to mastering an elephant. In the wild, this animal can pull up trees, trample crops, and endanger the lives of other beings. It is the strongest of all animals and can be very

211

dangerous. However, with sufficient skill, a person could capture and train this wild elephant, harnessing all its power. Then when the master says, "Walk," the elephant will walk; when the master says, "Sit down," the elephant will do so. Our negative emotions are just like this wild beast, powerful and dangerous when uncontrolled. They are difficult to master but with effort and determination, we can do it. Then when we want to concentrate on something, we can concentrate one-pointedly. When we want to visualize something, we can visualize clearly. And when it comes to viewing emptiness, we can do so without difficulty.

Of course we must have skillful methods to subdue the emotions. There are many techniques for developing these skills. We examined several of the techniques in the chapter on visualization. The shamatha techniques of following the breath, the vipasyana technique of analyzing the nature of mind and the arising of thought and consciousness, the tantric techniques of deity yoga, and the Nyam-shak or "equalizing" meditation are each very effective methods of training the mind and subduing the emotions.

No matter what technique we practice, we must have the proper physical and mental attitude. Proper posture of the body during meditation is essential. The seven positions recommended by Vairocana are legs in the lotus position, back straight as an arrow, hands tucked in at the hip joint, chin tucked in to the throat, shoulders lifted and rounded forward like eagle's wings, tongue on the roof of the mouth, and eyes slightly open and looking down the nose toward the ground. It is mentioned by many yogis that each facet of this posture has qualities that protect the mind from delusion.

The posture of the mind during meditation is also essential. The Six Dharmas of Tilopa teach us what to avoid so that the mind will be left clear. First, we are not to think of the past. There is no need to let the mind wander over past events and deeds, no need to laugh or cry over all that is finished. Second, we are not to think of the future. To imagine what might happen or try to make decisions is to produce more karma and habits without actually meditating. Third, we are not to think of the present. We might say, "Oh, now I'm really getting it," or, "Oh no, I made a mistake!" We get caught up in noticing our experiences and expectations. We try to fix our minds onto a certain sensation we have had or want to have. If our mind is in the past, future, or present, our meditation cannot be successful. Even if we could sit silently on our cushion all day, our meditation would be useless as we would simply be counting our illusions.

The fourth Dharma of Tilopa is that, when meditating, we should not meditate. This is not as contrary as it sounds. The nature of the mind is not meditating; the nature of the mind is emptiness. It is just as it is. There is no special object of meditation. As soon as we think, "I am meditating," then comes the thought, "I should be careful not to miss the meditation." Real meditation does not involve the concept of meditation as something separate from the natural state.

The fifth Dharma of Tilopa is not to analyze the mind during meditation. One should not question whether this is correct or incorrect meditation, or whether this is the right or wrong way to meditate, or even whether one is getting enlightened or not. One should not search the mind or analyze it to seek its nature.

The sixth Dharma of Tilopa is to let the mind be, clear and undistracted, absorbed in deep shunyata which is very clear and beyond all concepts.

After much practice, our meditation may become quite clear. At this time our teacher may begin to instruct us in the Mahamudra practices. There are four stages of Mahamudra practice and each stage has three levels, lesser, intermediate, and superior.

The first stage of Mahamudra is "one-pointedness." This means that whatever we concentrate on, we have no other single thought but that one. The lesser level is when we can concentrate one-pointedly with effort. The intermediate level is when the concentration still takes some effort but once we begin focusing, it is easy. The superior level is when one-pointed concentration is effortless.

The second stage of Mahamudra is "beyond conceptualization." The means that we are free from thought. Again there are three levels of facility: the lesser, in which concentrating beyond conceptualization requires effort to achieve; the intermediate in which once we begin concentrating, it is easy; and the superior, in which focusing beyond conceptualization is effortless.

The third stage of Mahamudra is "one taste." This means that samsara and enlightenment are perceived to be the same. This lack of dualism demands extremely pure perception. The three levels of practice are the lesser, requiring effort to achieve; intermediate, requiring initial effort to reach a state of ease; and superior, requiring no effort at all.

The fourth Mahamudra stage is "nonmeditation." At this point, there is no more learning or practicing. The lessons have been learned, and waking, sleeping, walking, talking, joking, and eating are all meditation. The lesser and intermediate levels are achieved by bodhisattvas; the superior level of effortless nonmeditation is the accomplishment of the fully enlightened being.

It is important to note that all Mahamudra practitioners begin at the bottom of this "ladder," which is lesser-level one-pointedness. To be able to concentrate one-pointedly with effort is well within the reach of ordinary students who want to do this practice and have a strong connection to a teacher who has meditation experience. All students progress step by step from "one-pointedness" through the three levels of "beyond conceptualization" and so on. The great bodhisattvas have followed this same path toward the same goal, the effortless nonmeditation of the fully enlightened.

However, most of us are unable to begin our meditation practice with clear visualizations or the ability to dissolve them into emptiness. We cannot start with the stages of Mahamudra because our concentration cannot be developed instantly. Sometimes even when we watch our breath, it can be difficult to keep our focus there. It would be easy for us to say, "Buddha must have made a mistake with this technique." Actually the problem is not the technique, but the fact that our mind is unstable due to a lack of accumulation of merit, and our understanding is poor due to a lack of accumulation of wisdom. These problems can hinder us in any technique we try, so we should not blame the method or the teacher.

We can address the lack of merit and wisdom through the Preliminary Practices. Prostrations and the Vajrasattva mantra purify body, speech, and mind; mandala offerings accumulate merit and wisdom; and Guru Yoga practice transforms wisdom from the guru. We need to come through this practice step by step. We cannot expect to jump from very little accumulation of merit and wisdom to a complete understanding of emptiness. These preliminary practices are very profound. The sage Milarepa said that if you have done this purification and understand it, meditation will not be difficult.

When meditating, we are actually looking at the mind. First we see a thought arise and we know it comes from the mind. When we look at the mind, we find that it has no substantial existence. It has no shape, color, form, or location. The nature of the mind is emptiness itself. Our thoughts have no form and come from the mind. Therefore our thoughts come from emptiness.

However, usually we deceive ourselves by believing that

our thoughts are substantial. That self-deception leads to actions and karma. An easy way to remind ourselves that our thoughts are nonsubstantial is to think of a sound that attracts us, like the ringing of a bell, and a sound that repels us, like pounding on a door. We are attracted to one sound and repelled by another, yet we have deceived ourselves if we believe either sound has any substantial existence. We cannot see sounds or touch them; they are nonsubstantial. When we listen to these sounds, we are viewing emptiness.

As we can see, there are many techniques that could lead us to the Mahamudra realization. The Buddha taught these different methods because people differ in their levels of merit and wisdom. If we can learn just one technique precisely, we will not need to learn them all.

After this discussion of how to realize emptiness, we must not think that it is nothingness. What is "there" is the Three Kayas, Dharmakaya, Sambhogakaya, and Nirmanakaya. "Kaya" is a Sanskrit word meaning "body," although this word does not denote a physical form. Unfortunately, human language does not have a more precise word for what is meant. Dharmakaya refers to the Truth Body, Sambhogakaya refers to the Enjoyment Body, and Nirmanakaya to the Emanation Body. The Three Kayas are the pure enlightened forms of mind (Dharmakaya), speech (Sambhogakaya), and physical body (Nirmanakaya). Our ordinary physical body, speech, and mind are impure forms of the Three Kayas. Negative actions of our physical body, speech, and mind lead us further into samsara, while positive actions on our part will lead us, level by level, to enlightenment. When we realize emptiness, we will know the Three Kayas.

Dharmakaya is the state of emptiness. It is not a state of being asleep or drugged or senseless. Realization of emptiness is a state of clarity and understanding. As Nagarjuna taught, holding to existence is bad and holding to nonexistence or nothingness is worse. We must walk the Middle Path.

Sambhogakaya is luminosity and Nirmanakaya is unimpeded wisdom. Calling Sambhogakaya luminosity means that all appearance is clear and brilliant just as it is. Calling Nirmanakaya unimpeded wisdom means that, while there is appearance, there is no obstruction to its luminosity because there is no clinging to it. These Three Kayas are difficult to grasp by just reading about them or hearing their description. It is only through learning to meditate step by step, without error, that we can increase our experience and understanding of the Kayas.

There is a story in the sutras about a student of the Buddha's who had been a famous guitar player before becoming a monk. He was given teachings on meditation by the Buddha but after much practice he was frustrated by his lack of realization. He approached the Buddha to find out what was wrong. "I've put much effort into meditating as you have taught. I have no wrong views to hinder me since I realize that you are fully enlightened. I think I just am not able to attain realization."

The Buddha inquired as to the monk's occupation in earlier life. When he learned that the man had been a guitar player, he said that he thought that work was more difficult than meditating. "When you play the guitar and the strings are too tight, does it sound good? Or when the strings are too loose, does it sound good?"

The monk replied that the guitar will not sound good if the strings are too tight or too loose. When the Buddha asked him how to make the guitar sound its best, the monk answered, "The strings must be neither too tight nor too loose, but somewhere in the middle."

The Buddha said, "That's how you need to make your mind when you meditate—not too tight or too loose, but somewhere in the middle. If you think you are plagued by illusion and try to concentrate very hard, your mind will be too tight. If you just let your mind wander, laziness arises and this means your mind is too loose. In the middle you can watch your mind and view emptiness." The monk realized the nature of the mind from the example of the guitar strings and was enlightened.

A great Tibetan lady teacher, Machik Labdrün, who was an incarnation of the Prajna Paramita, gave a similar Maha-mudra instruction to her disciples. "Tight, too tight; loose, too loose," is interpreted to mean that the mind should be concentrated just enough to avoid laziness and loosened just enough to avoid fixation.

The students of this teacher addressed her as "mother" and she referred to them as her "blood sons." These titles show the depth of respect and devotion possible between teacher and student. In the Kagyupa lineage, the relation-ship between devotion and the practice is compared to the relationship between the head and the body. Practice without devotion is like a human body that has lost its head; devotion without practice is like a head without a body. Either extreme is useless in pursuing enlightenment.

The sage Milarepa is an example to us of the student's devotion. Whatever his teacher told him to do, he did. If he had difficulty, he always questioned himself rather than his teacher, because he knew that the teacher has the wisdom to understand and utilize the student's karma. Through his devotion, Milarepa received the blessing of his teacher and was able to survive twelve years in a retreat on a mountain without any food.

After becoming enlightened, Milarepa had students of his own. As one student was leaving to do a retreat, Milarepa called him back for a last teaching. After the student had bowed to show respect to his teacher, Milarepa apparently changed his mind and sent him away. Soon he called the student back and then changed his mind again. When he called the student back for the third time, he saw how deeply devoted the student was and how eager he was to do whatever was required to receive this teaching. Milarepa told him no special preparations were needed for this teaching. Milarepa turned around and showed his buttocks, which were as hard as rock, to the student. This was a result of meditating for years. He told the student, "This is the deepest teaching I've ever given you. If you put this much diligence into your practice, you will realize enlightenment." The student recognized the compassion and wisdom of his teacher and committed himself to the same diligent practice. He, too, achieved enlightenment and had many students of his own. The combination of the skill of the teacher and the devotion and practice of the student makes enlightenment possible for us all.

Throughout this chapter, we have looked at the idea of emptiness and some ways to attain a view of it. Each of the Three Vehicles which the Buddha taught describes many techniques to achieve undistracted concentration and a view of emptiness. I have here given a brief and simple description of these various approaches and tried to suggest something of that view. No amount of reading, however, can lead to a true understanding of emptiness. We must put our efforts into developing our practice and our devotion to our teacher. This is our only real hope for attaining the perfect realization of emptiness.

Questions

The Dharma of Tilopa that says, "Don't meditate," confuses me. Would you say something more about this idea?

When you are learning meditation, you will have to concentrate on something and this will be the case for a long time. When you get to a mature stage of discipline and practice, you won't need to watch your mind as much, because it is no longer so active and negative. This is what Tilopa meant by "not meditating." The realization of this goal comes when you no longer need the tools.

Sometimes people have blissful experiences when they are not even practicing a spiritual path, and sometimes people have these wonderful experiences within the first weeks or months of embarking on a path. Is this their past karma?

If the person is not practicing a spiritual path, it is hard to explain. Maybe they take drugs or they don't sleep for many days and then these things happen.

If a person is starting a spiritual practice, then their glimpses of luminosity, emptiness, and deep peace come from the blessing of their teacher. This is actually not unusual. The new student has suddenly recognized a lifetime of desire for the connection with a teacher. When it is realized, all the student's devotion meets the teacher's siddhi, or accomplished knowledge, and the student has a taste of clear meditation or compassion or whatever the teacher deeply knows.

Certainly if the student does not continue to practice, the experience cannot be repeated, because it is not the student's own accomplishment. It is a great gift from the teacher but the gift will never be a substitute for the student's own practice. Your teacher will not carry you to enlightenment!

Will you talk about objectless compassion? Why should we cultivate compassion without an object for it?

You think "objectless" means "no object"? Here it means that you have compassion for no *particular* object, that is, you have equal compassion for all objects. Usually you have different feelings about things—some you love, some you hate, and some you ignore. These are the three poisons of desire, hatred, and ignorance at work. You feel great compassion for those things you love and no compassion for everything else.

To have objectless compassion means you feel equanimity toward all objects. All beings equally deserve your compassion because all beings suffer.

How does objectless compassion arise out of emptiness?

This kind of compassion grows alongside emptiness. They are inseparable, like the sun (emptiness) and sunlight (compassion). This kind of compassion is not like saying, "I love you." That expresses a feeling which varies with the object. Objectless compassion is limitless and it is a natural companion to emptiness which is unimpeded by particular objects.

When I sit down to meditate, it is difficult to avoid thinking about all the "forbidden" things in the Six Dharmas of Tilopa. My mind runs to think about the past or future or present and so on. It is actually easier for me to meditate naturally during daily activities. Is this all right?

Your mind is too tight. Just listen to your mind. If you let it relax and don't push any particular thoughts out, the "forbidden" thoughts will become boring and fade away.

Shouldn't we try to make daily life the meditation instead of formally meditating?

Your mind is too loose! If you never do a formal meditation, it is easy to think that everything is okay when it's not. The discipline of meditation gives you a contrast to daily life and reminds you that it really is samsara.

Conclusion

Some people have great knowledge of the Buddhist philosophy and views; I do not compare to them. However, I have written this book in the belief that it will be helpful to people who are interested in Buddhism.

The essential meaning of this whole book is that first you must train the mind to be calm and abiding in peace and clarity. This is most important before going on to other stages of the path. In order to attain calm abiding, one must rely on one's actions of the speech, mind, and body. If you perform wrong actions, it disturbs your tranquility and stirs the mind which then becomes very muddy. So you must first avoid wrong actions of speech, mind, and body. Then you can practice the right actions of speech, mind, and body, which will eliminate the obscurations of the mind and clarify it. For example, if you say unpleasant things about someone, this is a negative action of speech. You can see that it confuses, hurts, or develops negative emotions in another; this is a cause of your own confusion and destroys your calm abiding. If, on the other hand, you say pleasant things, this is called right speech and makes the other person calm and clear. This supports the development of a stable and calm mind. In general, this is an example of how one should watch one's actions to develop and sustain calm abiding.

In particular, for those who practice the Mahayana and Vajrayana, such practices as Nyung Nes are very effective for purification and cause the attainment of calm abiding. For example, during a Nyung Nes you take the eight Precept Vows for twenty-four hours; keeping these precisely and practicing the Mantrayana results in the purification of your speech, mind, and body. This comes about through engaging your body in Deities' Yoga, your speech in reciting mantra, and your mind in concentrating on deities which are nonsubstantial like a rainbow in the sky. The deities are the inseparability of appearance and voidness. Beyond this, there are many other techniques, such as the four extraordinary foundations (Ngöndro) and the traditional Three Year-Three Month Retreat, which accomplish real purification.

While training on this path, one must have a spiritual teacher. First it is important for the student to examine the teacher, and the teacher to examine the student to be certain that this is an appropriate connection and relationship. After having taken teaching from and meditated under the guidance of such a teacher, one should maintain devotion and stability in continuing to practice under that teacher. If you allow yourself to be led by your own desire, you will never find satisfaction. If you go from teacher to teacher without a stable practice, and spend your life without any goal, you will have great regret when you come to the end of your life. So you should have faith in one teacher and follow that teacher's instructions to gain some benefit from your practice in this life.

This does not mean you should not respect other teachers or other lineages, but one-pointed faith and devotion will protect you from experiencing an overweening desire for teachings that may confuse and hinder you on the path. For example, if you have one cup of tea in which you want to put all kinds of delicious foods that you desire, such as orange juice, sugar, apples, and peanut butter, that one cup of tea will be completely ruined. In order to have a fine cup of tea you must add just the appropriate ingredients. Then you can enjoy a good cup of tea and avoid getting an upset stomach. In the same way you should not mix all the various teachings and many different teachers together, but stay devotedly with one teacher and on one path that is right for you.

It is best not to criticize but to trust your teacher. What you receive from your teacher is most important. You should see the way you view your teacher as a reflection of your own qualities. Finding fault with your teacher is due to the darkness of this age and your own negativity and obscurations. In this dark age it is very rare to find a teacher as precise and pure as the Buddha; but if you find one, the delusion of finding fault with your teacher is remedied by seeing this fault or deficiency as a reflection of your own mind in a mirror.

Through the blessings of my lineage and my Root Guru, and my own sincere wishes, may this simple book benefit all sentient beings without exception. May virtue increase and all that is fortunate flourish.

Glossary

This glossary has been compiled in the hope of assisting readers who seek a brief definition of unfamiliar terms. The Tibetan term has been provided in parentheses. The reader should note that these terms, unlike those provided in the text proper (which are phonetic transliterations), are here given in their strictly orthographic form. It is hoped that this will benefit those who have, or who will come to have, a knowledge of the Tibetan alphabet and language. It is also hoped that this will not cause any undue confusion for the beginner.

ACCUMULATIONS, TWO The first is the accumulation of merit (Tib: bsod-nams-kyi-tshogs) which means exerting oneself in dharma practice and relinquishing ego-clinging, thereby creating the favorable conditions for following the path. The second is the accumulation of wisdom (Tib: ye-shes-kyi-tshogs) which is the result of the first accumulation. The realization of emptiness spontaneously arises out of compassion.

AVALOKITESVARA (Tib: spyan-ras-gzig) The bodhisattva of compassion who, without leaving the peace of meditative concentration, is continually active throughout the past, present, and future worlds in guiding sentient beings to the peace of Buddhahood, never ceasing until the whole of samsara is emptied.

BODHICITTA (Tib: byang-sems) There are both relative and absolute Bodhicitta. Relative bodhicitta arises from the practitioner's meditation upon and generation of compassion for other sentient beings (see BODHISATTVA). This leads to glimpses of absolute Bodhicitta, the true nature of reality, all-pervasive and effortless compassion for all beings. In turn, this inspires more compassion for beings and the intent to deliver them from samsara.

BODHI MIND (see BODHICITTA)

BODHISATTVA (Tib: byang-chub-sems-dpa') "Pure enlightened attitude." In general, this term applies to anyone who has

227

taken the vow to relinquish their personal enlightenment in order to work for the benefit of all sentient beings. More specifically, it designates a special class of beings who have not only taken that vow but who also have attained a significant level of realization.

BUDDHA (Tib: sangs-rgyas) The word has two parts in Tibetan, "sangs" and "rgyas" respectively. The first means clear and unstained by the defilements of attachment, aversion, and ignorance. The second refers to the attainment of all-pervasive wisdom. Normally we think of the word as denoting the historical Buddha, Shakyamuni, but it is just as often used to refer to the principle of enlightenment which all beings possess.

CHENREZIG (see AVALOKITESVARA)

COMPASSION (Tib: snying-rje) The essential motivation for all activities of the bodhisattva is compassion which arises from experiencing the suffering of sentient beings. Compassion is the basis for Dharma practice in the Mahayana and Vajrayana traditions.

CONFLICTING EMOTIONS (Tib: non-mongs) (see OBSCURATIONS) One of the two classes of obscurations (Tib: sgrib-pa), these stem inevitably from the belief in "me" and "mine" and the resulting emotional reactions.

DAKINI (Tib: mkha'-'gro-ma) "One who goes in the sky." It refers to certain female meditational deities or yidams. It can also describe female celestial messengers and protectors or female bodhisattvas who are performing actions for the benefit of sentient beings.

DEITY (Tib: lha) Arising from the Buddha's infinite compassion and wisdom, deities may take peaceful or wrathful forms in accordance with the individual personality and the great variety of mental states represented by sentient beings. As the object of a practitioner's meditation, they subdue mental and emotional defilements on the path to enlightenment.

DHARMA (Tib: chos) In general, Dharma means all phenomena in samsara and nirvana. Samsaric Dharma is the behavior or action which leads in the negative direction and causes one to sink in samsara. Nirvanic or Holy Dharma is divided into two types, the Dharma of Realization and the Dharma of Precept, and it leads one to enlightenment. It also refers to the body of teachings presented by the Buddha.

DHARMADHATU (Tib: chos-kyi-dbyings) All-encompassing space in which all phenomena of any sort arise and fall, without beginning or end.

DHARMAS, SIX OF TILOPA The six special techniques taught by Tilopa to realize mahamudra. (see Section III, Chapter 5: Viewing Emptiness)

EMPTINESS (see SHUNYATA)

ENLIGHTENMENT (see BUDDHA)

GOD (Tib: lha) Those beings who reside in the "god realms." There are numerous classes of gods including seventeen form and four formless categories. It is important to realize that from a Buddhist perspective, these gods are still in samsara, are not enlightened, and will ultimately fall to lower realms. (see REALMS, SIX)

GURU (Tib: blama) "Master, teacher." Although in English this word has come to refer to any teacher or monk, technically it refers only to enlightened masters.

HABITUAL TENDENCIES (Tib: bag-chags) The patterns of conditional response which arise from the residue left by all past ego-oriented actions over many past lifetimes. A response thus generated leaves its own karmic residue and the cycle continues through many future lifetimes.

HINAYANA (Tib: theg-chung) Also known as the Theravaden, the Hinayana is comprised of the paths of the Sravaka and Pratyeka Buddhas. Sravakas (literally meaning "hearers") concentrate on renouncing the world and pacifying the emotions. Through an understanding of basic Buddhist doctrines such as the Four Noble Truths, Pratyeka Buddhas (literally meaning "solitary Buddhas") concentrate on individual liberation through examining the Twelvefold Chain of Interdependent Origination in order to achieve Arhathood.

INTERDEPENDENT ORIGINATION (Tib: brtan-'bral) The interconnectedness of all actions and events as detailed in the teachings of the twelve interdependent links. In the Mahayana school especially, meditating on this teaching is considered to be an antidote to ignorance.

JEWELS, THREE (Tib: dkon-mchog-gsum) The three objects of refuge: Buddha, Dharma, and Sangha. (see BUDDHA, DHARMA, SANGHA)

KARMA (Tib: les) "Action." The law of karma is the doctrine of action and result. This holds that all experience down to the minute details is the result of previous action, and all future conditions are determined by what we do in the present. Virtuous actions lead to better states of existence; nonvirtuous actions lead to more suffering and unpleasant states.

KAYAS, FOUR (Tib: sku-bshi) "Four Bodies." It refers to the three bodies or modes of existence of Buddhahood, the three manifestations of the nature of enlightenment. The **Dharmakaya** or Body of Truth, is beginningless, centerless, and endless, completely indivisible, stainless, and concept-free. The **Sambhogakaya** or complete Enjoyment Body, is the perfect expression of enlightenment as radiant form, insubstantial and rainbow-like, whose spontaneous compassion and diligence accomplish the perfect liberation of beings. The **Nirmanakaya** or Emanation Body, is the compassionate embodiment of enlightened mind in a substantial though apparitional form which is perfectly skilled in continually establishing worldly beings on the path to peace, maturing them, and bringing them to their enlightenment. As Nirmanakaya, the Buddha may take form as a human who eats, sleeps, and shares daily life with students.

The latter two are called *form kayas,* and both abide in the Dharmakaya just as form abides in space. All three kayas are permanent in that the Dharmakaya is continuous with no beginning and no end, while the two form kayas are constantly present in samsara to express and hold the true Dharma and, out of perfect compassion, to completely fulfill their vow to benefit beings. They have perfect knowledge, being free from believing in a duality of samsara and nirvana. They always experience supreme bliss and, though they act in the world, they are unblemished by worldly characteristics.

These three kayas are conceived of as relating to the body, speech, and mind. Dharmakaya is the mind of the Buddha, enlightenment itself; the Sambhogakaya is the speech of the Buddha; and the Nirmanakaya is the physical form of the Buddha. In the Vajrayana, the root guru's body, speech, and mind are regarded as the Three Kayas.

A fourth kaya is the *Svabhavikakaya* (Tib: ngo-bo-nyid-kyi-sku), or Essence Body. It is the essence or unity of the first three kayas. It is said to be immeasurable, unaccountable, inconceivable, incomparable, and perfectly, ultimately pure.

LEVELS, TEN (Tib: sa-bchu) Stages of development a bodhisattva passes through on the path to enlightenment.

MADHYAMIKA (Tib: dbu-ma) The Mahayana school of the middle way. Founded by Nagarjuna and based on the second series of teachings given by the Buddha at Vulture Peak, it stresses the doctrine of emptiness while avoiding the extremes of eternalism and nihilism.

MAHAMUDRA (Tib: phyag-rgya-chen-po) Literally means "great seal," or "gesture." This is the meditative tradition passed down especially by the Kagyu school from Vajradhara Buddha to Tilopa and down to the present lineage holders. It is a state in which all experiences are transformed into wisdom and skillful means. From the union of these arise the empty, luminous, and unimpeded experience of enlightenment.

MAHASIDDHA (Tib: grub-thob-chen-po) In general, this term can refer to an accomplished or enlightened being. More specifically it is often used to denote one or all of the eighty-four mahasiddhas who became accomplished through the Vajrayana practices taught by the Buddha. The origins of Tibet's great tantric traditions can be traced to these eighty-four mahasiddhas.

MAHAYANA (Tib: theg-pa-chen-po) "Greater Vehicle." This vehicle is founded on teachings presented by Shakyamuni on Vulture Peak in northern India to an assembly of Buddhas, Bodhisattvas, and Arhats. These teachings go beyond the individual liberation emphasized by the Hinayana schools and teach a greater vision based on the emptiness of all phenomena, great compassion for all sentient beings, and acknowledgement of the universal buddha nature. The great hero of the Mahayana is the Bodhisattva who lives in the world solely to deliver all sentient beings from suffering and guide them to the supreme bliss of Buddhahood.

MANDALA (Tib: dkyil-'khor) Literally means "circle" or "sphere." A symbolic representation of a meditation visualization, usually taking the form of a palace with one or more deities present. Mandalas are traditional offerings for one's guru and are often imagined to be limitless in size, number, and splendid qualities.

MANTRA (Tib: sngags) Mantras are Sanskrit words or syllables, expressing the essence of various energies. Mantra protects the concentration of mind and is always done in conjunction with visualization, which is performed according to the prescriptions of a sadhana explained by one's guru. (see SADHANA)

MANTRAYANA (Tib: sngags-kyi-theg-pa) Another term for Vajrayana, whose systems of meditation use mantra extensively.

MERIT (Tib: bsod-nams) The karmic result of virtuous action. Since it is taught that all actions without exception have results, merit is the potential result derived from positive or virtuous actions. Without sufficient merit, the practitioner is unable to have certain experiences on the path. Thus a great deal of emphasis is often placed on accumulating merit sufficient for rapid progress on the path to enlightenment.

NATURAL STATE (Tib: gnas-lugs) Synonymous with "suchness." A term used particularly in Mahamudra teachings, it refers to the basic nature of enlightened awareness—fresh, unconditional, and spontaneous.

NGÖNDRO "Preliminary." It is used to describe the four extraordinary practices traditionally done at the beginning of a student's Dharma practices. They consist of 100,000 prostrations, Dorje Sempa Mantras, mandala offerings, and prayers to one's guru or lama; their purpose is to purify the body, speech, and mind of the individual in order to realize the Mahamudra stage.

NYUNG NES "Residing with less." This refers to limiting one's activities of body, speech, and mind to only those which generate an enlightened attitude and ultimate liberation of all beings. Specifically it refers to the two-day meditation retreat performed every month during the full moon.

OBSCURATIONS (Tib: sgrib-pa) There are two classes of obscurations: conflicting emotions, stemming inevitably from the belief in "me" and "mine"; and primitive beliefs about reality, i.e., believing that the objects of experience are substantial and possess an independent existence.

PARAMITA (Tib: pha-rol-tu-phyin-pa) Perfection, literally "gone to the other shore." It is styled as such because it carries us across the ocean of samsara to enlightenment. It is the supreme practice of the Mahayana, the Bodhisattva's method of relating to relative phenomena as a practice of the Buddhist path.

POISONS (see REALMS, SIX)

PRAJNA (Tib: she-rab) "Knowledge/awareness," "natural wisdom." Prajna is the awareness that discriminates while also seeing through conceptualization. This wisdom recognizes the impermanence and lack of inherent reality of phenomena, and its perfection is the direct seeing of things as they are.

PRAJNA PARAMITA (Tib: shes-rab-kyi-pha-rol-tu-phyin-pa) The sixth paramita, it is the awareness that all phenomena are without basis or origination. It transcends all duality, even those between existence and nonexistence, and between samsara and nirvana. Prajna Paramita is called the "Mother of All the Buddhas." The Prajna Paramita sutras describe prajna and the other perfections.

PRATYEKA BUDDHA (see HINAYANA)

PRECEPTS, EIGHT (Tib: so-sbyongs-yön-lag-brgyed-pa) These are the Mahayana precepts which practitioners often vow to uphold during retreats, such as Nyung Nes. Taking such a vow is a way of protecting or guarding the mind from creating negativities of body, speech, and mind, and from the problems of suffering which arise from a mind engaged in negative activities. Keeping the precepts restrains the negative mind from arising and prevents the increase of negative karma. These eight precepts include four root vows and four branch vows. The four root vows are to avoid killing, stealing, sexual misconduct, and telling lies. The four branch vows are to fast from food and beverages, to avoid intoxicants, to avoid sitting on a high throne or large bed, and to avoid using perfumes, wearing ornaments, singing, and dancing. Atisha added two more precepts when he went to Tibet to teach: abstaining from eating meat, and keeping the mind concentrated on the matter at hand.

RAINBOW BODY (Tib: 'ja'-lus) This is one fruit of a yogi's practice. Having completely transformed physical experience into the basic space of Dharmadhatu, he/she maintains an apparent body during the lifetime while at death his/her body may dissolve into rainbow-like luminosity.

REALMS, THE SIX (Tib: 'gro-ba-rigs-drug) Literally means the "six destinies." These are the six possible destinies of sentient beings caught in the cycle of samsaric existence. The higher realms are those of the gods, jealous gods, and humans. The lower realms are those of the animals, hungry ghosts, and denizens of hell. Each realm is characterized by a predominant poison: pride (god), jealousy (jealous gods), desire and aversion (human), ignorance (animal), greed (hungry ghost), and anger (hell). The human realm is considered the most fortunate of these because only here does a being have the opportunity of altering its situation by cutting off the cycle of samsara.

REBIRTH (see SAMSARA)

REFUGE (Tib: skyabs) The basis and foundation of one's entire practice as a Buddhist is taking refuge in the Buddha, the enlightened one; in the Dharma, the teachings; and in the Sangha, the community of experienced bodhisattvas and fellow practitioners. In the Vajrayana, in addition to these Three Jewels, one takes refuge in the Lama as the root of all blessings, the Yidam as the root of all accomplishment, and the Dharma protectors as the root of enlightened activity. (see ROOTS, THREE and JEWELS, THREE)

ROOTS, THREE (Tib: rtsa-gsum) The Three Roots in which the Vajrayana practitioner takes refuge (in addition to the Three Jewels). They are the Lama and lineage as blessing root or source of blessings, the Yidams as the root of accomplishment, and the Dharma protectors as the root of enlightened action, i.e., pacifying, enriching, magnetizing, and destroying. The root guru embodies all three.

SADHANA (Tib: sgrug-thabs) A Vajrayana ritual text setting out a particular meditation practice.

SAMADHI (Tib: ting-nge-'dzin) Describes a one-pointed involvement in meditation where the object of meditation and the practitioner are experienced as inseparable and indistinguishable. While there are many kinds of samadhi, it is important to note that the term does not infer anything about the subject's realization or accomplishment.

SAMADHI GOD (Tib: samten-gyi-lha) There are many different classes of gods, including the samadhi gods of which there are four types. Clinging to one's samadhi experience results in birth as a samadhi god, where one's attachment to samadhi is likely to grow. Thus it is tainted with conflicting emotions and is not pure. Ultimately this in turn leads to exhaustion of the good karma which originally led to birth as a god, and the individual falls to one of the lower realms.

SAMAYA (Tib: dam-tshig) The Vajrayana principle of commitment in which the disciple binds his/her whole experience to the path, extending the point of view of Dharma to every activity. The most important samaya is to maintain a proper attitude toward one's root guru.

SAMSARA (Tib: khor-ba) Samsara is the cycle of rebirth, the wheel of existence, arising out of ignorance and marked by suffering. (see REALMS, SIX)

SANGHA (Tib: dge-'dun) In the broadest sense, the term refers to the whole community of practitioners from monks, nuns, and lay people to the assembly of enlightened bodhisattvas. The Sangha is one of the three objects of refuge, the Three Jewels.

SHAMATA (Tib: zhi-gnes) "Calm abiding." This term denotes both the method of meditation to achieve tranquility and the meditative state that is its result.

SHUNYATA (Tib: stong-pa-nyid) This is the doctrine that all concepts and phenomena are empty of any reality and that self and other are egoless. Shunyata is like space, unborn and unceasing.

SKANDAS, FIVE (Tib: phung-po-nga) Skandhas are sometimes referred to as the five "psycho-constituents of reality." They are form, feeling, perception, intention, and consciousness, and together they comprise an individual's total life experience. When they are purely perceived or transcended (or transformed, in the Vajrayana), each one is related to one of the five Buddha families.

SRAVAKA   (see HINAYANA)

SUCHNESS   (Tib: de-kho-na-nyid) Things as they are.

SUTRA   (Tib: mdo) Texts in the Buddhist canon attributed to Shakyamuni Buddha. They are usually dialogues between the Buddha and one or more of his disciples, elaborating a particular topic of the teachings.

SVABHAVIKAKAYA   (See KAYAS, FOUR)

TANTRA   (Tib: rgyud) This word has many ramifications, but basically it refers to those systems of meditation described in the root texts of the Vajrayana. Tantra itself means "continuity." This refers to the continuity maintained throughout one's practice from the basic ground or foundation, along the path, and through to complete fruition of the practice. This continuity is one's own Buddha nature and identification of one's body, speech, and mind with the Three Kayas.

TANTRAYANA   (see VAJRAYANA)

TRUTHS, TWO   (Tib: bdan-po-nyid) These are relative truth (Tib: kun-rdzob-kyi-bden-pa) and absolute truth (Tib: don-dam-pa'i-bden-pa). Relative truth is the truth of the ordinary world, normally overlaid with mistaken perceptions and projections based on ego-clinging and the belief in phenomena as substantially real. Seen from the point of view of someone purified of ego-clinging, this self and these phenomena are all an illusion. Absolute truth is the profound experience of reality as neither existing nor not existing; as empty, undefiled, unbiased, unchanging, joyful, and complete. From the enlightened point of view, relative and absolute truths are actually inseparable.

VAJRA   (Tib: rdo-rje) Adamantine, diamond-like, indestructible; the thunderbolt. Vajra means that which is indestructible, i.e., that which is beyond arising and ceasing.

VAJRAYANA (Tib: rdo-rje-theg-pa) "Diamond or Indestructible Vehicle." This vehicle is based on the teaching of the Shakyamuni manifesting in the form of Vajradhara, the Dharmakaya Buddha. They consist mostly of oral and secret teachings passed from teacher to disciple. There are two classes of these oral teachings, one for gifted students capable of instantaneous enlightenment and a second delineating a graded path of instruction in which the student passes from one stage to the next, coming gradually to enlightenment. Because the Vajrayana presents the practitioner with the actual fruition of wakefulness and suchness, it is called the "quick" path. It is said that one practicing the Vajrayana can achieve Buddhahood in a single lifetime.

VEHICLES, THREE (see HINAYANA, MAHAYANA, and VAJRAYANA)

VIPASYANA (Tib: lhag-mthong) Seeing beyond; superior or excellent seeing; insight. A meditative technique which identifies and analyzes the patterns of the mind and the world it projects, achieving a state of clear-seeing which expands into perfect knowledge.

WISDOMS, FIVE (Tib: yes-shes-lnga) These are the wisdoms of the five buddha families which the individual achieves through the transformation of the five poisons. They include: 1) Mirror-like wisdom, 2) Discriminating awareness, 3) Wisdom of equanimity, 4) All-accomplishing wisdom, 5) Dharmadhatu wisdom.

YIDAM Literally, "yi" means "mind" and "dham" means "tight." This refers to a strong mental connection with deities (see DEITY); more particularly, this word is associated with personal meditational deities.

Bibliography

Batchelor, Stephen, trans. *A Guide to the Bodhisattva's Way of Life* by Shantideva. Dharamsala, Library of Tibetan Works and Archives, 1979.

Guenther, Herbert V., trans. *Jewel Ornament of Liberation* by sGam-po-pa. Boulder, Shambala, 1971.

Gyatso, Geshe Kelsang. *Meaningful to Behold.* London, Wisdom Publications, 1983.

Hanson, Judith, trans. *The Torch of Certainty* by 'Jam-mgon Kong-sprul. Boulder, Shambala, 1977.

Lodö, Venerable Lama. *Bardo Teachings, The Way of Death and Rebirth.* San Francisco, KDK Publications, 1982.

Lodö, Venerable Lama, trans. *Maintaining the Bodhisattva Vow and the Bodhicitta Precepts,* Second Edition. San Francisco, KDK Publications, 1984.

Mates, Marion, trans. *Entering the Path to Enlightenment* by Shantideva. London, Allen & Unwin, 1970.

McLeod, Kenneth, trans. *Writings of Kalu Rinpoche.* Vancouver, Kagyu Kunkhyab Chuling, 1976.

Colophon

This book was phototypeset in Garth and Novarese Ultra by Connie Kudura, ProtoType, Eugene, Oregon. Production assistance by Imageworks Design & Illustration/Barbara Bryan Cooper, Eugene, Oregon.

The text was printed on 55-pound Theta Natural paper and the cover was printed on 100-pound Delta Diamond Coat. Printing and binding were done by Delta Lithograph Co. of Van Nuys, California.

 The symbol of KDK Publications is the Tibetan letter "ah" which symbolizes the unborn, formless Dharmakaya.